America's Spiritual Capital

Other works of interest from St. Augustine's Press

America's Spiritual Capital

Nicholas Capaldi
and
Theodore Roosevelt Malloch

ST. AUGUSTINE'S PRESS
South Bend, Indiana
2012

Manufactured in the United States of America

1 2 3 4 5 6   17 16 15 14 13 12

Library of Congress Cataloging in Publication Data
Capaldi, Nicholas.
America's spiritual capital / Nicholas Capaldi
and Theodore Roosevelt Malloch.
p. cm.
Includes index.
ISBN 978-1-58731-037-9 (paperbound: alk. paper) 1. United States
– Religion. 2. Religion and politics--United States. 3. Economics –
Religious aspects. 4. Christianity – United States. 5. Judaism –
United States. I. Malloch, Theodore R. II. Title.
BL2525.C358 2012
201'.720973 – dc23   2012011287

∞ The paper used in this publication meets the minimum requirements of
the American National Standard for Information Sciences - Permanence of
Paper for Printed Materials, ANSI Z39.48-1984.

St. Augustine's Press
www.staugustine.net

For all those down the centuries
who have given their lives, limbs, and livelihood
for the American experiment in liberty.

CONTENTS

AMERICA'S SPIRITUAL CAPITAL
INTRODUCTION

This book tells a story, a story about America's spiritual capital. America has created the greatest civilization the world has ever known, and it has done this because of its spiritual capital, the values and beliefs by which individual Americans have interpreted and transformed the world.

The book is comprised of six chapters. Chapter One outlines the concept of 'spiritual capital.' Building on Putnam's notion of 'social capital,' a comprehensive account is provided of the interrelationship among human, social, and spiritual capital, and how these relate to the larger world.

In Chapter Two there is a generic account of the Judeo-Christian heritage and shows in what sense it has served as a form of spiritual capital.

In Chapter Three we document the extent to which the Judeo-Christian heritage has historically served as the spiritual capital of America. Of special importance in this chapter will be the articulation of how Judeo-Christian spiritual capital has been the source of the spiritual quest of modernity, how that quest has evolved into globalization, and why America, because of its spiritual capital, has been able to provide leadership for that quest. The larger thesis is that America is by virtue of its specific spiritual capital heritage not only the beneficiary of its advantages but also the leading exemplar of the spiritual quest of modernity. It is because America is engaged in a spiritual quest that it can exercise world leadership as opposed to domination and oppression.

Chapter Four will focus exclusively on the economic consequences of America's spiritual capital. Specifically, we examine the extent to which economic development, growth, and entrepreneurship depend on spiritual capital. Religious beliefs have a measurable impact on individuals, communities, and societies. It is not a coincidence that the *Spiritual Capital Initiative* of the John Templeton Foundation reflects the philanthropic impulse of a major American entrepreneur.

Chapter Five does for political freedom what Chapter Four did for economic freedom. The major thesis of this chapter is that there is a symbiotic relation between America's spiritual capital and our political institutions and freedoms. The argument here is that the substantive spiritual vision supports the political and economic procedural norms of a free society. The procedural norms are not otherwise defensible. Whereas Chapter Three makes a purely historical case, Chapters Four and Five make the case that America's success and leadership have an integral relation to its spiritual capital.

Like any form of capital, spiritual capital may lie dormant or be wasted, it may be used productively, it may be augmented, and it may be diminished or eroded. In Chapter Six we see how the heritage is under assault from a variety of sources and what happens when scientific, technological, economic, and political institutions are detached from their spiritual roots. The result is a natural progression from governmental bureaucratic centralization to secularism to reductive materialism and ultimately to a social-collectivist conception of human welfare. Within the story there is an argument, namely, that these achievements will not be sustained without that heritage, and for all of the above reasons the heritage needs to be reaffirmed. We argue that the future of modernity, globalization, and America depends on the extent to which there is a reaffirmation of America's spiritual capital.

In the pages that follow we will explain the meaning and importance of something we call 'spiritual capital.' We will identify the unique content of America's Judeo-Christian spiritual capital. We will show how each has in many ways come to define America. In the process we shall also identify the origins and sources of the current attacks on Judeo-Christian spiritual capital. These include most notably:

a. Perennial (heretical) utopian Christianity (Gnosticism), now in the form of Christian and other forms of Socialism

b. Rousseau/Marx-derived narratives of equality and complaints about Modernity

c. Militant Secularism (domestic + international) and,

d. Militant Islam (international)

In the chapters that follow we rebut these attacks. We argue that America will not survive without a renewal of its Judeo-Christian spiritual capital.

a. Specifically, this means the importance of personal autonomy and responsibility stemming from the dignity of the individual as a human person, and,

b. The need to support civil association with a robust content-full morality.

At no place will we be advocating a theocracy or anything less than a democratic Republic that is rooted in commerce and, ultimately, produces human flourishing. We will however be advocating the rejuvenation of Judeo-Christian spiritual capital as a cultural phenomenon, the non-apologetic expression of one's faith, the re-education of misguided clerics, educators, the media, and America's leaders, and most of all direct, honest, lawful, and vigorous confrontation of America's critics and its enemies.

Tradition tells of a chime that changed the entire world when it rang on July 8, 1776. It was the sound from the tower of Independence Hall summoning the citizens of Philadelphia to hear the first public reading of the Declaration of Independence by Colonel John Nixon.

The Pennsylvania Assembly had ordered the Bell in 1751 to commemorate the 50-year anniversary of William Penn's 1701 *Charter of Privileges*, Pennsylvania's original Constitution. It spoke of the rights and freedoms valued by people the world over. Particularly insightful were Penn's ideas on religious freedom, his stance on American rights, and his inclusion of citizens in enacting laws. The Liberty Bell gained iconic importance when abolitionists in their efforts to put an end to slavery throughout America adopted it as a symbol. As the Bell was created to commemorate the golden anniversary of Penn's Charter, the quotation, *"Proclaim Liberty throughout all the land unto all the inhabitants thereof,"* taken from Leviticus 25:10, seemed particularly apt.

This book rings that same Bell again and defends and rearticulates America's spiritual capital.

CHAPTER ONE

SPIRITUAL CAPITAL

"When we have reconstructed the whole of mundane history it does not form a self-explanatory system, and our attitude to it, our whole relationship to the human drama, is a larger affair altogether – it is a matter not of scholarship but of religion. . . . Ultimately our interpretation of the whole human drama depends on an intimately personal decision concerning the part we mean to play in it." – Herbert Butterfield.[1]

Introduction

Samuel Huntington, in his book *Who Are WE?*, noted that "America was founded by British settlers who brought with them a distinctive culture . . . the English language, Protestant values, individualism, religious commitment, and respect for law. The waves of immigrants that later came to the United States gradually accepted these values and assimilated into America's Anglo-Protestant culture." However, our national identity according to Huntington is being eroded.[2] There are a

---

1   *Christianity and History* (1949), pp. 27 and 86.
2   Samuel P. Huntington, *Who Are WE?* (New York: Simon & Schuster, 2004), book cover. See John Howard's book, *Christianity: Lifeblood of America's Free Society (1620–1945)*. See also *The Puritan Gift* by Kenneth and William Hopper (2009).

number of other related challenges not alluded to directly by Huntington. We believe that the religious dimension of this crisis is crucial and needs to be emphasized, and it is for that reason that we focus on the concept of "spiritual capital."

America's spiritual capital consists of the fundamental values that have made possible its unparalleled economic, social and political achievements. We believe that the Judeo-Christian heritage is at the core of those values. The general purpose of this chapter is to elaborate for the reader the concept of spiritual capital.

It is also our purpose to legitimate the importance of the concept of "spiritual capital." This purpose is necessary only because of the misguided prevalence among academic and media elites of a belief in the intellectual superiority of scientism and of secular humanism and who have a dismissive attitude toward those who sincerely subscribe to religious beliefs and practices. We challenge this prejudice by exposing how shallow, flawed and intellectually indefensible the prejudice is. We address that issue in Chapter Six.

Definition of Spiritual Capital

Spiritual capital refers to our most fundamental beliefs concerning who we are and the meaning of our lives, with special regard to how those beliefs relate to our professional careers and the economy.

A large part of our lives is focused on some relatively small and specific tasks. Every once in a while, however, we all try to see the big picture.[3] What does it all mean? Not only every individual but every organization, every culture, has to answer the big questions: "Who are WE?" "What is the world all about?" and "How do we relate to the world, both human and physical?" Our answer to those questions constitutes our spiritual capital.

---

3   This is what a German scholar would call "Weltanschauung."

Why do we call this "capital"?

We are accustomed to thinking of "capital" as a purely financial resource in the same way that we are accustomed to thinking of property as real estate. Just as we have come to understand that there are many different kinds of property, including intellectual property, we have come to recognize that there are many different kinds of capital. Adam Smith, the founder of modern economics, distinguished among different kinds of capital: financial capital (traditional sense), human capital (abilities and skills of workers), and social capital (social networks and relationships). All of these are potential resources that factor into the production of wealth. Put simply, and following Francis Fukuyama's usage, social capital consists of norms shared among members of a group that permit cooperation among them.

One particular set of shared norms that has been highly influential are religious or spiritual beliefs. Max Weber, the sociologist who authored *The Protestant Ethic and the Spirit of Capitalism*, provided the landmark exploration of the relation between religious belief and economic and political activity. Weber contended that our consciously held beliefs were the real causes of why people behave as they do. Spiritual beliefs were among the most important such beliefs. *According to Weber, those who worked hard because they saw themselves as doing God's work in the world were inspired to become more creative and economically successful.*

Sociologists have continued to focus on "social capital." The World Bank (1985) made it the basis of a research program. James Coleman was responsible for popularizing the concept in the 1990s when he published "Social Capital in the Creation of Human Capital."[4] Nobel prize-winner Gary Becker made the concept crucial for economic theory in *Accounting for Tastes (1996)*. Social capital, most notably, became the center of

4 *American Journal of Sociology (1988).*

attention in Robert Putnam's *Bowling Alone* (2000). The importance of social capital for corporate action in particular and business life in general was stressed by Cohen and Prusak (2001) in *In Good Company*.

Why do we call this "spiritual"?

Broadly speaking, "spiritual" capital is that aspect of social capital linked with religion and/or spirituality: *the effects of spiritual and religious practices, beliefs, networks and institutions that have an impact on individuals, communities and societies.*

As a beginning, it might be helpful to distinguish between the notions of "doing" versus "being." Modern society and its organizations have created conditions where individual identity and spirit are masked by an emphasis on "doing" things while deemphasizing the nature of people's "being." But, history has shown us that a genuine spirit anchored in an ethical, values-based system has been the sustaining force of individual innovation and personal character throughout the ages.[5]

Earlier we said that spiritual capital provides answers to three important questions essentially about how we are going to lead our lives. An answer to these questions is not a material fact about the world; rather it is an intimately personal decision concerning the part we mean to play in the world. To the extent that we choose to see meaning in the world or our relationship to it, we reflect something "spiritual." From this point of view, spiritual capital is the big picture that informs a culture so that all other institutions must be viewed from its perspective rather than vice versa.

An individual freely chooses meaningful ways of understanding himself/herself and the world. We must use our imagination in order to learn. It is the unique ordering of our experience in imagination that makes us individuals. One of the most

5   Charles Murray, *Human Accomplishment*, Part IV, (pp. 385–458).

important ways in which we utilize our imagination is in reconstructing the thought of other persons. In the beginning we reconstruct the thoughts of those around us, our initial cultural exposure. Our initial epistemology is social – it is only through interaction with our cultural inheritance that we become who we are. What is important for us to recognize is that the cultural inheritance is not a rigid structure; rather, the inheritance is recreated through its appropriation. The metaphor of "inheritance" is useful here for many reasons. An inheritance may be preserved in its exact form, it may be squandered and lost, it may grow in predictable fashion, or it may be invested and developed in ways that were not foreseen. It is in this sense that a culture might die, grow, or be a fertile source of adaptation. Extending the metaphor, *the cultural inheritance might be profitably viewed as a form of capital.*

Although spiritual capital is typically viewed as a form of social capital, we maintain, on the contrary, that *spiritual capital is not a mere subset of social capital but is in fact more encompassing.* Spiritual capital encompasses both human capital and social capital. It provides the overarching structure that defines human and social capital. It is the grand narrative that defines a group, any functioning group. It is important then to resist the temptation of the social scientist to see spirituality simply as a reflection of religion and religions as mere institutions within a larger social structure of institutions. From this point of view, spiritual capital is the grand narrative that informs a culture so that all other institutions must be viewed from its perspective rather than vice versa.

The diagram on page 6 is taken from Malloch and Massey:[6]

Spiritual capital is not identical to a specific theology or a set of specific religious beliefs and practices. Various religions may reflect spiritual capital in varying degrees and ways, but spiritual capital may be reflected outside specifically religious institutions and by people who do not consider themselves as strictly religious.

---

6   Malloch and Massey, Renewing American Culture (2005).

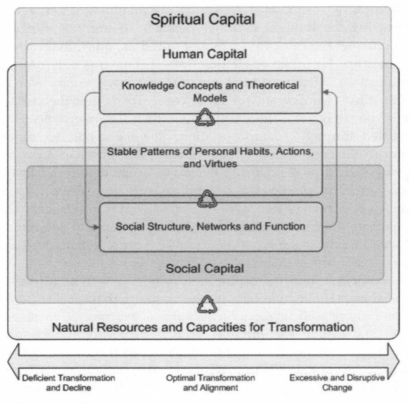

History has shown us that a genuine spirit anchored in an ethical, values-based system has been the sustaining force of individual innovation throughout the ages. For any one person, spirituality can be a noun – a state of being where one connects, sees the whole, and self-actualizes. Likewise, spirituality can be a verb that connotes the journey into one's self to bring meaning to life. The journey can take a number of paths (religion, therapy, community, etc.) of which faith-based religions are prominent today. Thus, our view is that spirituality is not necessarily synonymous with any particular religious devotion but that spiritual strivings are important to creating the whole person.

Despite these qualifications, it is our contention that spiritual capital rooted in religion provides the deepest and most sustainable conceptual base for spiritual capital. Spiritual capital is "the fund of beliefs, examples and commitments that are transmitted from generation to generation through a religious tradition, and which attach people to the transcendent source of happiness . . . we are moral beings, in all the ways that Adam Smith describes. But we are also spiritual beings. We seek out the transcendent source of our values. We join with others in acts of worship and prayer. Through spiritual discipline, habit and exercise, we absorb the legacy of spiritual knowledge that is contained in a religious tradition."[7] The difference between social capital and spiritual capital is that the former is built through social interaction whereas the latter "comes from another relation altogether than the relations of human society: the relation with God."[8]

Spiritual capital might seem at first sight to be antithetical to popular conceptions of a free market system and thus not of much concern for those focused on market share and return on investment. Wilhelm Röpke's *A Humane Economy* (1957) provides us with this insight:

> Self-discipline, a sense of justice, honesty, fairness, chivalry, moderation, public spirit, respect for human dignity, firm ethical norms – all of these are things which people must possess before they go to market and compete with each other. These are the indispensable supports which preserve both market and competition from degeneration. Family, church, genuine communities, and tradition are their sources.[9]

Likewise, Charles Handy in his book *The Age of Paradox* writes to this point:

> We misinterpreted Adam Smith's ideas to mean that if we each looked after our own interests, some "invisible hand" would mysteriously arrange things so that it all worked out for the best for all. We therefore promulgated the rights of

7   Theodore Roosevelt Malloch, "Spiritual Capital and Practical Wisdom," *Journal of Management Development*, vol. 29, No. 7/8 (2010), p. 756.
8   Ibid., p. 758.
9   See Theodore Malloch, *Spiritual Enterprise*, dedication page.

the individual and freedom of choice for all. But without self-restraint, without thought for one's neighbor and one's grandchildren, such freedom becomes license and mere selfishness. Adam Smith, who was a professor of Moral Philosophy, not of Economics, built his theories on the basis of a moral community. Before he wrote *The Wealth of Nations* he had written his definitive work, *A Theory of Moral Sentiments*, arguing that a stable society was based on "sympathy," a moral duty to have regard for your fellow human beings. The market is a mechanism for sorting the efficient from the inefficient, it is not a substitute for responsibility.

Spiritual capital, then, is the marriage of two seemingly opposing forces – the drive for profit and the nourishment of the human spirit. As Mitroff & Denton write, "spirituality may well be the ultimate competitive advantage." The paradox disappears once one understands that spirituality is not necessarily a passive retreat from the world but the active re-creation or co-creation of a better world.

As Pope John Paul II put it,

> Man is made to be in the visible universe an image and likeness of God himself, and he is placed in it in order to subdue the earth. . . . In carrying out this mandate every human being, reflects the very action of the Creator of the universe. . . . Organizing such a productive effort . . . taking the necessary risks . . . an essential part of that work [is] initiative and entrepreneurial ability. . . .
>
> . . . The original source of all that is good is the very act of God, who created both the earth and humankind, and who gave the earth to humankind, so that we might have dominion over it by our work and enjoy its fruits (Gen 1:28). God gave the earth to the whole human race for the sustenance of all its members, without excluding or favoring anyone. This is the foundation of the universal destination of the earth's goods. The earth, by reason of its fruitfulness and its capacity to satisfy human needs, is God's first gift for the sustenance of human life. But the earth does not yield its fruits without a particular human response to God's gift, that is to say, without work. It is through work that we, using our intelligence and exercising our freedom, succeed

in dominating the earth and making it a fitting home. In this way, one makes part of the earth one's own, precisely the part which one has acquired through work; this is the origin of individual property. Obviously, one also has the responsibility not to hinder others from having their own part of God's gift; indeed, one must cooperate with others so that together all can dominate the earth. . . . In our time, the role of human work is becoming increasingly important as the productive factor both of nonmaterial and of material wealth. Moreover, it is becoming clearer how a person's work is naturally interrelated with the work of others. . . .

. . . It is precisely the ability to foresee both the needs of others and the combinations of productive factors most adapted to satisfying those needs that constitutes another important source of wealth in modern society. Besides, many goods cannot be adequately produced through the work of an isolated individual; they require the cooperation of many people in working towards a common goal. Organizing such a productive effort, planning its duration in time, making sure that it corresponds in a positive way to the demands which it must satisfy, and taking the necessary risks – all this too is a source of wealth in today's society. In this way, the role of disciplined and creative human work and, as an essential part of that work, initiative and entrepreneurial ability becomes increasingly evident and decisive.[10]

Spiritual Capital in America: A Preview

Virginia was perhaps the most important colony that debated religious freedom. The Anglican/Episcopal Church was established in that colony from inception and it took many years to arrive at its disestablishment. Freedom of religion was both a core American spiritual and political value, as most of the settlers to America – from Puritans in Massachusetts to Episcopalians in Virginia to Quakers in Pennsylvania to Presbyterians in New Jersey to Baptists and Methodists in

10   *Centesimus Annus*, paragraphs 31 and 32.

Georgia – came to these shores to have a place where they could worship freely. [11]

Thomas Jefferson drafted *The Virginia Act for Establishing Religious Freedom* in 1779 three years after he wrote the *Declaration of Independence*. The act was not passed by the General Assembly of the Commonwealth of Virginia until 1786. Jefferson was by then in Paris as the U.S. Ambassador to France. A group headed by Patrick Henry, who sought to pass a bill that would have assessed all the citizens of Virginia to support a plural establishment, resisted the Act. James Madison's *Memorial and Remonstrance Against Religious Assessments* was, and remains, a powerful argument against state-supported religion. It was written in 1785, just a few months before the General Assembly passed Jefferson's religious freedom bill.

Some revisionist Colonial scholars have in recent years argued that America is not a Christian nation and that the Founders were largely not believers. This is a blatant falsehood. The range of denominational associations were many and Deists were very prominent among them, but Christian faith in one form or another formed the very backbone of American beliefs and in many ways shaped the entire culture, its formation and the conception of this Republic.[12]

---

11   This needs to be qualified somewhat. True religious freedom developed in most places in the wake of the Revolution. Some colonies (e.g., Massachusetts) were mostly unfree with respect to religion. It is more accurate to link religious freedom to the ideas gestating in the colonies and given expression in the Revolution, and to the experience of religious pluralism in colonies such as PA and NY.

12   Thomas S. Kidd, *God of Liberty: A Religious History of the American Revolution* (New York: Basic Books, 2010). See all Thomas G. West, *Vindicating the Founders*: Race, Sex, Class, and Justice in the Origins of America (Rowman & Littlefield, 2001). George Washington *Farewell Address*: religion is the "indispensable support" of "political prosperity."

CHAPTER TWO

JUDEO-CHRISTIAN SPIRITUAL CAPITAL

"As an exercise in perfectionism, Christianity cannot succeed even by its internal definitions; what it is designed to do is to set targets and standards, raise aspirations, to educate, stimulate and inspire. Its strength lies in its just estimate of man as a fallible creature with immortal longings. Its outstanding moral merit is to invest the individual with a conscience, and to bid him to follow it. This particular form of liberation is what St. Paul meant by the freedom men find in Christ. And, of course, it is the father of all other freedoms. For conscience is the enemy of tyranny and the compulsory society; and it is the Christian conscience which has destroyed the institutional tyrannies Christianity itself has created. . . . The notions of political and economic freedom both spring from the workings of the Christian conscience as a historical force; and it is thus no accident that all the implantations of freedom throughout the world have ultimately a Christian origin." – Paul Johnson, *A History of Christianity*, p. 516

Introduction

We will from time to time speak of *Judeo-Christian* spiritual capital. We have several reasons for doing so. First, Christianity developed historically as a reform movement within Judaism.

Second, Christianity continues to incorporate elements of Judaism, specifically the *Old Testament*. Third, there are two fundamental and seminal values shared by Judaism and Christianity, namely *liberty* (Exodus) and *equality* (Genesis). With regard to these values, we shall argue below and later that (a) these values are fundamental to American spiritual capital, (b) there is an ongoing and perhaps permanent tension between liberty and equality that helps to explain many conflicts in modernity and in America, (c) that these values when held substantively motivate individuals to support the procedural norms of political life, and that (d) the absence of these values in the origins of Islam makes it more difficult for many Muslims and others to feel comfortable with American-style political practices.

We also wish to make the following disclaimers. Some readers will object to the expression "Judeo-Christian." They might see some sinister attempt to absorb Judaism into Christianity or to deny important differences between Judaism and Christianity. Our use of the expression has no such objective. Moreover, there cannot be an authoritative, systematic and definitive articulation of specifically Christian doctrine because (a) Christianity has evolved over 2000 years and continues to evolve, (b) it has split into many divisions, and (c) its major doctrine is that God and God's will are beyond total human comprehension and articulation. Nor are we going to provide an account of all the theological controversies that have evolved over time. Finally, we are not going to enter into all of the philosophical puzzles raised by Christian doctrines. The major philosophical insight that provides a space for all religion and religious narratives including Christianity is the inability to which we alluded earlier, namely, the inability to provide an alternative comprehensive philosophical or scientific account of the world. It suffices for our purpose to present a generic narrative that was and is believed by most of those who call themselves Christians and that has historically provided a way of life that inspires them.

Judeo-Christian Spiritual Capital

With specific regard to its application to America, the core of Judeo-Christian spiritual capital consists of the following:

* * Divine origin of the universe
* * God has given purpose and meaning to the universe
* * The creation of human beings in God's image
* * The ultimate dignity of individual human beings
* * An eschatology that can help us to realize the destiny of human beings in the world
* * We fulfill God's plan and redeem ourselves in work ("Man ought to imitate God, his creator, in working, because man alone has the unique characteristics of likeness to God," and "Man shares by his work in the activity of the creator" – John Paul II, *Laborem Exercens* (Para. 25)
* * Toleration

Some of the ways in which these core beliefs worked themselves out in subsequent Western history are as follows.

Christian World View and Narrative: God & Creation

The ultimate explanation for everything is the inscrutable will of a supernatural and divine person we know as God. God is both transcendent (Psalm 90:2, Romans 1:20) and immanent. God has from time to time communicated to the human race through the prophets. These events are commemorated in the *Old Testament*.

God created the natural world we know as the physical universe (*Genesis*). The world also has a history – His Story (or narrative). This idea is a unique intellectual contribution. The classical Greeks and Romans had a cyclical conception of time – the world is a process that repeats itself endlessly; wisdom is recognizing and acquiescing in where one is in the cycle. The Judeo-Christian narrative has a conception of time we refer to as Biblical (i.e., exemplified in the Bible). This means that history has a beginning, middle, and an end. History is progressive,[1] and it is precisely this progress that offers us the possibility of hope. The end of history comes about with the fulfillment of God's purpose.

We cannot overemphasize the importance of this *eschatology*, the narrative that helps us to realize the destiny of human beings in the world. Hinduism and Buddhism do not discern any purpose or meaning. According to the Tao, the universe has no personal or meaningful relation to human beings. Taoism, Confucianism, and Shinto do not have a meaningful eschatology that can help us to realize the destiny of human beings in the world. Most non-European languages do not have a word for "freedom." We do not see the resources outside of the Judeo-Christian inheritance for dealing with global culture.[2] Moreover, the Judeo-Christian narrative is self-critical, strives for universal-

1   Stark, op. cit., p. 9.
2   Richard Madsen is Distinguished Professor & Chair of the Department of Sociology at the University of California, San Diego. He is the author or co-author of eleven books on Chinese culture, American culture, and international relations. This E-Note is a slightly edited version of his Templeton Lecture on Religion and World Affairs, which he delivered in Philadelphia recently. "The secularization thesis is a pillar of modern social theory. There are different versions of this thesis, but all hold that religion will fade away and/or become irrelevant to public life in the modern world. In some countries, secularization is not only the basis of a descriptive theory but of normative policy. Chinese government policy toward religion is explicitly based on both the descriptive and normative aspects of the secularization thesis.

But many social scientists are now saying that the secularization thesis is wrong and that we need a post-secularist social theory to account for the empirically obvious facts of the early twenty-first century. Religious belief and practice have not faded away, and in many parts of the world they are playing a more obvious role in public life than in the past century. Religion, moreover, is dynamically evolving, taking on new forms as well as reviving old forms, and becoming intertwined with the modern bureaucratic state and the market economy in new ways. This leads to a crisis in modern social theory but also to crises in modern political practice.

In this article, I discuss how this crisis manifests itself in Chinese politics." For video and audio of this lecture visit: http://www.fpri.org/multimedia/20091026.madsen.religiouspolicychina.html

ity, and has as its great strength the power of assimilation. That is, it is a fertile source of adaptation of what can be absorbed from other historical cultures.

What we want to focus on is the extent to which Christianity played a crucial role in the development of modern science. In his monumental study, *Science and Civilization in China* (Cambridge, 1954–1984), Joseph Needham points out that during the Middle Ages the Chinese were far more advanced than the West in scientific matters. Nevertheless . . . the so-called scientific revolution occurred in the West and not in China. What is the explanation for this? According to Needham, what the Chinese lacked was "the conception of a divine celestial lawgiver imposing ordinances on non-human Nature. . . . It was not that there was no order in Nature for the Chinese, but rather that it was not an order ordained by a rational personal being, and hence there was no conviction that rational personal beings would be able to spell out in their lesser earthly languages the divine code of laws which he had decreed aforetime"(p. 581). In short, what the Chinese lacked was the Christian God. When we turn to Islam, we find that it could not harmonize scientific research and God.[3]

The cosmological role of God as it evolved in Western thought has been insightfully summarized by R.G. Collingwood in his *The Idea of Nature*. Specifically, Renaissance science took its idea of God from the Bible, namely, that *God is a transcendent Being who created the world as well as human beings in his own image, and moreover, that the created world is both knowable and benevolently disposed to human interests*. More specifically, "Renaissance natural science was based on the analogy between nature as God's

---

3   See H.F. Cohen (ed.), *The Scientific Revolution: A Historiographical Inquiry* (Chicago, 1994); G.E. v. Grunebaum, Islam: *Essays in the Nature and Growth of a Cultural Tradition* (Cambridge, 1969); A. Sayili, "The causes of the decline of scientific work in Islam," *The Observatory in Islam and Its Place in the General Theory of the Observatory* (Ankara, Turkey: 1960). See also *Inquiry and Analysis Series - No. 179*, June 11, 2004 No.179. The Alexandria Declaration: Arab Reform - Vision and Implementation.
4   R.G. Collingwood, *Idea of Nature* (Oxford, 1960), p. 9.

handiwork and the machines that are the handiwork of man."[4] In Galileo, in Descartes, and in Locke, "Nature, so regarded, stands on the one hand over against its creator, God, and on the other over against its knower, man. Both God and man are regarded as transcending nature; and rightly, because if nature consists of mere quantity its apparent qualitative aspects must be conferred upon it from outside, namely by the human mind as transcending it; while, if it is conceived no longer as a living organism but as inert matter,[5] it cannot be regarded as self-creative but must have a cause other than itself."[6] It is but a short step from this to the idea, program in fact, expressed by Descartes when he said that we are here "to make ourselves the masters and possessors of nature."

Human Freedom and Sinfulness

God also created humanity. He created the human race in his own image (Genesis 1:1). That is, human beings were given reason and imagination, but most importantly free will. The ultimate purpose and meaning of the universe are products of God's will. The ultimate dignity of human beings flows from the divine creation and purpose. It is for this reason that Christianity was ultimately responsible for ending slavery in Medieval Europe;[7] it was for this reason that with the Spanish conquest of the New World it was necessary to debate whether the natives ("Indians") could be enslaved; one side invoked Aristotle's notion of the natural slave, but the other side of the debate invoked the Christian idea that you can't enslave someone who has been baptized. The issue is not whether and how long slavery existed; the issue is not whether some people who identified themselves as Christians defended the institution of slavery; the issue is whether Christianity provided the framework within

---

5   Gaukroger, Stephen, *The Emergence of a Scientific Culture; Science and the Shaping of Modernity 1210–1685*. Oxford: Clarendon Press, 2006. pp. ix + 563.6

6   Ibid., pp. 102–3.

7   Early Christians had no political agenda. Christians could even be slaves. Slavery was thought to be a consequence of sin.

which other Christians could argue for and achieve abolition.

Classical Greek philosophy for all of its contributions is not the origin of the notion of individual human dignity.[8] Aristotle, for example, had no concept of the will. Again, wisdom for the classical Greeks was a matter of understanding and acquiescing in why things had to be the way they were. At most, we could restore things to their natural state. It is for this reason that St. Augustine rejected astrology! For Christianity, we fulfill God's plan and redeem ourselves in work. Part of this is conveyed in the notion that humanity is to have dominion over the rest of creation (Genesis 1:26).

We are free to love God and to live according to his will (1 Corinthians 13:2). But precisely because God gave human beings free will, human beings have the capacity to defy God or to assert their own will over against God's plan. Human sinfulness then is self-assertion against God.

Three misunderstandings need to be avoided. First, conforming to God's plan is not a simple matter precisely because the world exists through time and has a history and because His will is inscrutable. Clearly, there will be disagreements about the positive content of His will. On the other hand, we can be fairly certain of what is inconsistent with God's plan, and that is a world marked by the violation of the Ten Commandments. It would also be fair to say that utopia will not be achieved on earth (Tower of Babel) because of human sinfulness. That is one reason there is life after death. All forms of earthly utopianism are Christian heresies.

Second, acting in a manner consistent with God's plan is not a mere matter of social conformity. In order to fulfill God's plan, human beings need to be autonomous, that is, they must first know how to control themselves. Moreover, autonomous beings do not impose their will on others. One can see in Kant's various formulations of the *categorical imperative* secular restatements not only of the golden rule but of what it means to be a

8 Eric Voegelin, *New Science of Politics* (Chicago: University of Chicago Press, 1987).

free and responsible human being in the Christian narrative: Do not make an exception of yourself; treat other human beings as ends in themselves and not simply as means to your personal ends; act in a way which presumes that the ultimate ends of each individual are consistent with the ultimate ends of all other individuals (so-called kingdom of ends).

To assert oneself in opposition to God is to believe that (a) one lives in a zero-sum world, (b) that satisfying one's own interests takes precedence over satisfying the interests of others, and (c) that it is legitimate to satisfy oneself at the expense of others.

Let us give an example of how this plays out in two different sets of circumstances. In the medieval world the economy is agrarian and characterized by scarcity (zero-sum or worse – a declining supply of essential goods and services). Anyone who wants more can only get more at someone else's expense. To want more is to be greedy, that is, to want a larger share of a finite economic pie that can only be had at the expense of others. To want more than what you routinely or already have is to be "greedy." Contrast that with a modern industrial/technological economy where there is no potential limit to growth.[9] Those who want more and who are willing to pursue it – either more of the same or new and better goods and services – are people who expand the economic pie. To want more is to expand the pie for everyone even if the relative percentages of the economic pie do not change. Here the interests of each individual properly understood are consistent with the interests of all other individuals – a kingdom of ends!

This is one reason why it is important to stress the "will" and not just reason ("If I understand all mysteries and all knowledge . . . but have not love, I am nothing" – 1 Corinthians 13:2). If we have Free will → then we can choose how to respond; if we can choose how to respond then → we can exercise our imagination; if we can exercise our imagination then we are not a slave to our

---

9   Julian Simon, "Can the Supply of Natural Resources Be Finite?" in *The Ultimate Resource 2* (1996).

inherited cultural framework, so we can transcend any particular culture including our own; → if human beings can transcend their inherited culture then → it makes sense to engage in proselytism.

Third, choosing to love God or choosing to assert ourselves is not a one-time decision. It reflects an ongoing tension in human existence. It is why human beings need to remind themselves periodically of what life's purpose is, to rededicate themselves, and, of course, periodically to redeem themselves. This is one reason why the theme of redemption is so central to so much of Western literature, or at least it was before the narrative of protest focused exclusively on conflicts of class, gender and race.

Jesus Christ

Christians believe that the historical Jesus was the Messiah foretold in the *Old Testament*[10] and whose life is chronicled in the gospels. This is what is meant by the divine incarnation. It was Jesus's role, among other things, to suffer and die for our previous sins and thereby to reconcile humanity to God. Jesus accomplished this as well by the founding of the Church.

Doctrinal Evolution

Early Christians thought that the second coming of Christ and the end of history were imminent. When this turned out not to be the case, Christians had to provide a larger rationale for themselves and differentiate themselves from other sects. To do so, they turned to philosophy. For roughly the first millennium of its existence, Christianity turned primarily to Plato. During its second millennium, it turned at the beginning and subsequently to the newly discovered works of Aristotle.

It is important to note why the absorption of classical Greek

---

10   Jews and Muslims reject this contention.

philosophy was so crucial. First, the absorption of philosophy in general, and different philosophies at that, meant that *Christianity acquired the capacity for self-criticism and doctrinal evolution from its very beginning.* Throughout most of its history, Judaism remained juridical rather than philosophical in its intellectual orientation. Islam, on the other hand, remained much more rigid and far less self-critical and capable of doctrinal evolution.[11]

Second, as we shall see, it is not possible to understand subsequent history and even contemporary public policy debates without understanding that all sides to these debates reflect earlier debates within Christianity and the influence of classical thought in framing those debates. Third, like other traditions, Christianity does not speak with one voice. There have always been internal tensions within the tradition. For our purposes in this chapter it is not necessary to address or resolve those tensions but to identify them and to exhibit their ongoing influence. First we shall identify some of those tensions and then comment on the relevant influence.

The first tension with which Christianity has to grapple is its relation to the larger political and economic context. Christianity as a religion is focused on how living a life consistent with religious precepts helps us to achieve eternal salvation, i.e., salvation in the next life. Christianity began as a despised and minor sect within the Roman Empire. Early on, Christians recognized that they lived in a world that was not necessarily hospitable to its way of life. It is in this sense that Christianity must be understood first and foremost as a religion, not a political or economic theory. The religious focus on the transcendent trumps any political or economic institution; specifically, individual Christians must always act consistent with transcendent norms. Christianity, therefore, does not entail a particular economic or political agenda or arrangement. To the extent that Christians

11 *Inquiry and Analysis Series - No. 179* June 11, 2004 No.179; The Alexandria Declaration: Arab Reform - Vision and Implementation, Aluma Dankowitz.

take particular positions in specific contexts, they must not only act consistent with the transcendent norms but must also guard the liberty of the Church from outside political or economic domination. Christians must decide which public policies best preserve the independence of the religious life and the liberty of the Church. Inherent then in the conception of Christianity is the idea of a community set apart from but operating within a larger political and economic context. Recall here Christ's admonition according to Matthew, to "render therefore to Caesar the things which are Caesar's and unto God the things that are God's."

Throughout all of non-Western world history, and through most of Western history[12] (Greeks, Romans, medieval world), societies were organized as enterprise associations.[13] Enterprise associations have a collective goal to which the goals of individuals must be subordinated. In the ancient world, the concept of freedom applied to the city-state, if it was applied at all, not to the individual. Communities of all kinds (starting with the family) in the ancient world were enterprise associations.

Christianity as a religion conceived of itself in the beginning as an enterprise association. But Rome also conceived of itself as an enterprise association and as the all-encompassing political enterprise association. That is why no sharp distinction was made by both Greeks and Romans among religion, ethics, and politics.[14] Conflict and the persecution of Christians were inevitable. Subsequently, when Christianity evolved into not only a tolerated religion but the official religion of the Roman Empire, it was no surprise that Christianity conceived of itself as the ultimate enterprise association. As such, it felt obliged to persecute those who were not Christians. In this respect, it played a similar

---

12 When we speak of the "West," we have in mind that part of Europe historically and culturally defined by Roman Catholicism and subsequently Protestantism – as opposed to Orthodox Christianity.
13 Oakeshott, *On Human Conduct.*
14 Scholars still debate to this day what is the correct order of the chapters in Aristotle's two works entitled *"Ethics"* and *"Politics."*

role to Zionism (understood as an alternative to assimilation) and Islam. To this day, the vast majority of Muslims conceive of their society as an enterprise association. Islamic law covers every aspect of life, from issues of daily living to politics and governance. Islamic law does not distinguish between religion and state. The *ulema* function as both jurists and theologians.

But the Roman Empire would eventually collapse as the enterprise association of the West. The barbarian invasions soon reminded Christians that they lived in the world after the fall. It is at this point that St. Augustine becomes a crucial figure. Augustine drew upon the works of Plato. For Plato, the world is not self-explanatory but requires reference to an unseen ideal world. We thus inhabit two worlds at once. Actual social and political institutions are also to be judged by reference to an ideal world. The ideal is never achievable in this world (utopia is not realizable) but serves as a standard for judging the imperfections of this world and provides a standard that we strive to achieve, however imperfectly.

Augustine translated this into the doctrine of two cities.[15] There is the heavenly City or the City of God – ideally what the Church should be no matter what horrors surround us; there is also the City of Man or the City of the Devil – the political world with its monopoly on force and the world of apparently permanent international conflict. Christians must strive to maintain the purity and independence of the Church, but they must also accept that the state is a necessary evil. Whereas classical thinkers thought we could achieve fulfillment in political life, Augustine maintains that fulfillment comes only in the spiritual domain. The state does not have a positive function; it exists to combat evil. Hence it is legitimate for Christians to serve as Roman soldiers as long as they are not asked to violate their faith. Pacifists are utopian heretics who are unwitting accom-

---

15   See Christopher Dawson, "The Christian View of History," in Dynamics of World History, pp. 245–62 (ISI Books, Wilmington, DE, 2002).

plices or enablers of evil. One can already see in Augustine the later distinction within the Church itself between the Church visible and the Church invisible.

A second crucial feature of the Western Judeo-Christian heritage is expressed in St. Augustine's doctrine of the Two Cities. As Voegelin argued, Christianity de-divinized the classical state of Greece and Rome. Ultimate human fulfillment is to be found in the spiritual life devoted to God and not in the State. The State is a necessary evil. This will later be translated into the doctrine of limiting the power of the government; this is the origin of political freedom. The Hebrew prophets had initially played that role in their warnings to political leaders. This doctrine of Two Cities never found its way into Orthodox Christianity. As Lord Acton made clear in his discussion of the relationship between Christianity and freedom, the tension between the medieval Church and rising national monarchies is the origin of so many of the freedoms that liberal societies take for granted.

As a corollary to limited and limiting government, we note that one of the most persistent features of the Judeo-Christian heritage to be found in both the Old and New Testaments is the inviolability of private property. We are all by now familiar with the relationship between Christianity and the rise of capitalism.

Augustine was the dominant intellectual figure during the first millennium of Western Christianity, but he was not read or influential in the Eastern Mediterranean where Orthodox Christianity flourished. The East continued to subscribe to what later became known as the doctrine of Caesero-Papism – namely, that the head of the State was also the head of the Church, for example, in pre-revolutionary Russia. This helps to explain in large part why after the end of the Cold War and the fall of the Iron Curtain, some Eastern European countries had a much more difficult time adjusting to market economies and political freedom. Hungary, Poland, and the Czech Republic had much less difficulty, because their cultural heritage was tied to Rome. To this day, in countries like Romania, voters do not vote for individual candidates in elections but only for slates from different parties. The bitterness and horrors of the recent Bosnian War reflect, in part, the conflict between two enterprise associations rooted in Orthodox Christianity and Islam.

In his monumental *History of Christianity*, Paul Johnson sheds some light on this tension. Johnson contrasts a Church which strives to "embrace and reflect society, in the process of transforming it" and not "an alternative to society."[16] "The official church was conventional, orderly, hierarchical, committed to defend Society as it existed, with all its disparities and grievances. But there was also, as it were, an anti-Church, rebellious, egalitarian, revolutionary, which rejected society and its values and threatened to smash it to bits. It had its own tradition of revolutionary prophecy, inherited from the Jews. . . ."[17] Further, he points out that "basically all these heresies were the same. They aimed to substitute a perfect élite for the corrupt clergy."[18] Johnson offers interesting descriptions of medieval Christian egalitarian terror.[19]

So we have here two answers or two positions that will remain in constant tension: those who conceive of Christianity as purely a religion in an imperfect world and those who dream of Christianity as the ultimate and all-encompassing enterprise association, dominating every aspect of life. The Reformation and Counter-Reformation address this tension, but it is never fully resolved.

Eric Voegelin[20] in his *New Science of Politics* sees modernity as a reflection of Gnosticism. Gnosticism is the perennial Christian heresy of believing that paradise can be achieved on earth. To use Voegelin's expression, it is the *immanentization of the eschaton*. Historically it is found in the medieval period, in humanism, the

16 Johnson, p. 145.
17 Ibid., p. 255.
18 Ibid., p. 251.
19 Ibid., p. 262.
20 Voegelin shares the Weberian critique of positivism (scientism) in the social sciences.

Enlightenment, progressivism, liberalism, positivism, and finally in Marxism. It seeks to reverse Augustine's de-divinization of the state by creating a civil theology. Voegelin gives us a quasi-Augustinian account in which the transcendent is repeatedly lost sight of in history. The prognosis for Voegelin is not the prescription that we return to the insights of classical political philosophy. He maintains that Gnosticism is internally incoherent both because it represses the truth of the soul and its ineffectiveness in practice leads to an omnipotent state in which Gnostics cannibalize themselves. He instances Puritanism as a case study. At the same time, he sees America and England as a bulwark against Gnosticism precisely because they maintain the Mediterranean inheritance (Greek philosophy, Judaism, and Christianity). It is the explicit combination of philosophy and religion, not philosophy alone, that may be our salvation.

After the collapse of the Roman Empire, Christianity was the institution that provided Western Europe with its cultural and geopolitical identity. It preserved the classical heritage, converted the barbarian invaders, and gave some semblance of unity. It was during this time that Aristotle's works were rediscovered (via Muslims) and reintroduced into the West.

Aristotle viewed the cosmic order from a monistic (not dualistic) point of view; hence, the world is self-explanatory. For Aristotle, the world was one great chain of being understood from the perspective of teleological biology – everything had a purpose and each purpose fit into a larger framework of purposes. He applied this model to the social world as well. Hence, each institution has a goal; institutions form a *hierarchy* of goals; and the state (polis) is the supreme institution. By now, the reader should see that Aristotle lends himself to the notion that societies are enterprise institutions. Moreover, the political domain defined the ethical domain (opposite of Plato): to be good is to conform to the goal of the institution. One becomes good through habituation to the goal of the institution. In short, political institutions have a positive role to promote the human good by promoting good habits.

Let us summarize how the absorption of the classical inheritance framed this first tension for Christianity. The Greco-Roman model is that of the enterprise association in which no sharp distinction exists among religion, politics, and ethics. The Platonic model sees the actual world as an imperfect manifestation of the ideal world[21] and therefore sees the primary role of the state as preventing harm. The Church of the first millennium, especially in Augustine, conceived of the world dualistically – we are members of one ideal enterprise association (Church) interacting with the state in a fallen world in which the role of the state is negative – prevent harm. Early monasteries are modeled partly after the idea of philosopher-kings in Plato's *Republic* – no private ownership, no families, etc. – but it is not expected that the whole of society can be modeled this way.

In the second millennium the West was still under attack from barbarians to the north and Muslims to the South and East. Under the influence of Aristotle on St. Thomas Aquinas and others, and under the existential initial necessity of providing the unity that feudal rulers were unable to provide, the Church conceived of itself as the all-encompassing institution within the universal hierarchy and with the state or political domain as subservient to the Church. Having immersed itself now directly into the world of affairs, the state was then conceived of as having a positive role under the tutelage of the Church of promoting the good.

This, of course, is not the end of the story. Aristotle was rediscovered not only by the Church but by secular rulers as well, who saw themselves as presiding over the collective good of an enterprise association. What ensued were several centuries of conflict involving such things as the investiture controversy. This conflict was ultimately resolved in favor of national monarchies. The Reformation's contribution to this resolution is reflected in the Protestant return to Augustine's model. This is not to deny that there were Protestants who wanted a national Church

---

21 We agree with those scholars who maintain that Plato's Republic was not intended to be a blueprint of an actual society but an ideal.

to direct the state; nor is this to deny that there were and are Christians who still cling to the notion of a universal enterprise association having a collective good presided over by a clerisy.

What should not be lost sight of is Lord Acton's conclusion: "To that conflict of four hundred years [feudal hierarchy vs. ecclesiastical hierarchy] we owe the rise of civil liberty. If the Church had continued to buttress the thrones of the king whom it anointed, or if the struggle had terminated speedily in an undivided victory, all Europe would have sunk down under a Byzantine or Muscovite despotism. For the aim of both contending parties was absolute authority. But although liberty was not the end for which they strove, it was the means by which the temporal and the spiritual power called the nations to their aid . . . and England [got] her Parliament out of the alternative phases of the contest. . . . But the authority of religion, and especially of the papacy, was thrown on the side that denied the indefeasible title of kings."[22]

The achievement of political liberty will be directly related to the achievement of economic liberty – something we shall elaborate on in Chapter Four. For the moment it is worth noting that to the extent the state thinks of itself as an enterprise association it will demand and expect to control the economy. Note as well that the development of the notion of individual autonomy reinforces the notion that individuals be allowed to pursue their lifeplans with minimal government interference.

This leads us to a discussion of the second tension within Christianity, the relation of the individual to the institution. The Greco-Roman world had no clear conception of the will; hence it had no clear

---

22 Acton, "The History of Freedom in Christianity," p. 33, Vol. I – *Essays in the History of Liberty*, ed. Rufus Fears, LF, 1985, *Selected Writings of Lord Acton*. It was Acton as well who opposed Pope Pius IX's assertion of the doctrine of papal infallibility and who famously made the claim in a letter to Bishop Creighton in 1887 that "I cannot accept your canon that we are to judge Pope and King unlike other men with a favourable presumption that they did no wrong. If there is any presumption, it is the other way, against the holders of power, increasing as the power increases. Historic responsibility has to make up for the want of legal responsibility. *Power tends to corrupt, and absolute power corrupts absolutely.* Great men are almost always bad men." (Italics added.)

conception of the individual. Conceptually, individuals were analogized as species within a genus. The question was always, what do people who occupy my social role do? Neither Plato nor Aristotle had a notion of individuals who deliberately choose evil; for Plato, the dysfunctional person lacked the requisite degree of reason; for Aristotle, the dysfunctional person was not properly habituated. Once Christianity introduced the notion of a will that is free to choose, that changed everything. The ultimate existential and ontological reality was that of an individual (free) will. It would take some time for this idea to work itself out, but by the Renaissance and the Reformation a full blown conception of individualism had emerged.[23] "Through its early centuries, Christianity as practiced was not individualistic. . . . It was Christian theology itself that was potentially revolutionary, teaching that all human beings are invited into a personal relationship with God. . . . It was a theology that empowered the individual acting as an individual as no other philosophy or religion had ever done before."[24]

Crucial to our narrative is the rise of the notion of the sanctity of the individual and its later evolution into the rise of the modern individual. This notion is already present in embryonic form in "[St.] Paul's conception of the Church: a community where the spirit worked through individuals, rather than an organized hierarchy where authority was exercised by Office."[25] This is the insight behind the claim that "the other great faiths minimize individualism and stress collective obligations."[26] An enterprise society is total and compulsory – it cannot tolerate alternatives or dissidents, hence religious wars, second-class citizenship at best for non-believers, and the persecution of

23   Oakeshott, "The Masses in Representative Democracy," (1961), *Rationalism in Politics and Other Essays* (Indianapolis: Liberty Fund, 1991).
24   Murray, Human Accomplishment, p. 402. See also: L. Dumont, *Essays on Individualism: Modern Ideology in Anthropological Perspective* (Chicago, 1986); Deepak Lal, *Unintended Consequences: The Impact of Factor Endowments, Culture, and Politics on Long-run Economic Performance* (Cambridge – MIT: 1998).
25   Johnson, *op. cit.*, p. 48.
26   Stark, p. 31.

dissidents. Christianity has evolved out of that frame of mind; not so for other religious traditions such as Islam.[27] The crucial point to be made here is that while Christianity as well as Islam has had collectivist traditions, Christianity also has had within itself the resources for promoting individual freedom. It is not at all clear that this is so with Islam, and the impetus for change within Islam seems to come from external pressure.[28]

This second tension soon merges with the first. What is the relation of an autonomous individual soul to the collective enterprise of the Church? Moreover, what is the relation of that same individual to a political entity, namely, any State which claims to be an enterprise association? What emerges out of this set of conflicts is the notion of a *civil association*,[29] a form of association which does not have a collective goal to which individuals are subordinate, but an association with procedural norms which exists to serve the goals of the individuals who comprise it. One can still envisage a Church as an enterprise association within a larger political context of a civil association (shades of Augustine), but membership in the Church or any other enterprise association would be a voluntary choice with freedom of entry and exit.

Thus is born the contemporary notion of a *classical* liberal society as conceived by the American Founders in which the individual is supreme and the state is a necessary evil. But the alternative model never fully disappears, so in the contemporary world we have *modern* liberals for whom society is an enterprise association (family) and in which it is the role of the state to make us good.

---

27 The Islamic Brotherhood, the Taliban, and al-Qaeda advocate theocratic enterprise associations and terrorist attacks against the perceived threat of Western civil association. Critics of Islam include among many others Ibn Warraq, Daniel Pipes, and Dario Morera-Fernandez. Advocates of a liberal form of Islam claim that the sacred texts need not be read in the foregoing fashion – they include Fazlur Rahman Malik, Norman Daniel, and Carl Ernst among others.

28 Bernard Lewis, *What Went Wrong?* (2003).

29 Oakeshott, op. cit.

The third great tension is the relation of Christians of different sects to each other and to non-Christians. We know what the early answer is, namely, to the extent that Christians see themselves as part of an enterprise association they opt for domination over and persecution of those who do not belong to the enterprise. This is what all enterprise associations initially do. Over time, however, with memory of itself as an early persecuted sect, with the growing hostility to political enterprise associations, with the recognition that the Church itself is free as long as no sect controls the state, and with the gradual appreciation of the centrality of individual human dignity, Christians came to articulate a doctrine of toleration. To tolerate is not to legitimate an opposing point of view, but to agree not to persecute those who subscribe to it as long as they agree not to persecute you. The conceptual origin of this evolution was noted by John Locke who, in his essay *On Toleration*, argued that Christianity has the resources to promote toleration: you can only achieve salvation if you freely choose and love God – i.e., because you have free will – image of God. If I force you to pay lip service, then that of itself will not help to achieve your salvation. "The idea that religious liberty is the generating principle of civility, and that civil liberty is the necessary condition of religious, was a discovery reserved for the seventeenth century. Many years before the names of Milton and Taylor, of Baxter and Locke were made illustrious by their partial condemnation of intolerance, there were men among the Independent congregations who grasped with vigour and sincerity the principle that it is only by abridging the authority of States that the liberty of Churches can be assured. That great political idea, sanctifying freedom and consecrating it to God, teaching men to treasure the liberties of others as their own, and to defend them for the love of justice and charity more than as a claim of right, has been the soul of what is great and good in the progress of the last two hundred years."[30]

---

30   Acton, op. cit., p. 47.

Finally, it is worth pointing out that some of the earliest work on religious toleration is to be found in the writings of Milton and Locke. Both Milton and Locke argued that Christianity properly understood had the inner resources to make sense of religious toleration without degenerating into mindless relativism.

Three essential ingredients of Christianity here come together: universality, toleration, and limited government. While all religions serve as the basis of some morality and therefore support some form of civilization, only the Abrahamic faiths (Judaism, Christianity, Islam) espouse universality. Why is this important? All religions require moral behavior toward other members of the religious community, but only the Abrahamic faiths require it toward all of humanity instead of espousing a double standard. Within the Abrahamic faiths, only Judaism (prophets) and Christianity (Augustine) – properly understood – maintain a tradition of limited government. That is why toleration is unconditional in countries with a Judeo-Christian heritage. It is unconditional in the sense that no limitations or penalties are put upon members of other faiths or no faith as long as they too practice toleration. It is precisely for this reason that *only the Judeo-Christian heritage can serve as the foundation for a liberal globalization as opposed to totalitarian globalization or anti-globalization.*

The fourth great tension in Christianity is between liberty and equality. Christianity, as we have shown above, is the origin of the modern conception of liberty. Christian liberty resides in the recognition by the state of the independent status of the Church and that fulfillment comes within the spiritual domain.

Christianity is also the origin of the modern conception of equality. It asserted the equal moral worth of all persons in the eyes of God. The origin of this notion is in *Genesis* – all human beings "male and female" were created in the "image of God." Paul expressed it (*Galatians* 3.26–29) as, "There is neither Jew nor Greek, there is neither bond nor free, there is neither male nor female: for ye are all one in Christ Jesus." This view was repeated in *Colossians* 3:10–11. In the early Church, Christians maintained the classical conception of hierarchy. Clergy were distinguished from lay people because the sacraments needed to be administered by someone in a theologically superior position.

With the advent of modernity equality played a more central role. As we shall see in the next chapter, the Aristotelian teleological, organic and hierarchical conception of the universe was challenged in science, religion, morals, and politics. The idea of natural political hierarchies, both within the Church and in the secular political sphere, was challenged. The Protestant attack on the hierarchical notion of the Church was expressed by Luther in *To the Christian Nobility* (1520), "It is pure invention that popes, bishops, priests and monks are to be called the 'spiritual estate'. . . . There is really no difference. . . . [i]t is intolerable that in the canon law so much importance is attached to the freedom, life, property of the clergy. . . . Why are your life and limb, property and honor so free, and mine not? . . . Whence comes this great distinction between those who are equally Christian? Only from human laws and inventions!" Calvin went on to assert that authority derives from voluntary agreement among equals to submit – first in the organization of the Church and then in the political sphere. Anabaptists like Thomas Münzer went further and asserted complete social equality, to be achieved by violence if necessary.

Summary

The evolution of the Christian narrative makes possible the following:

1. Belief in progress and hope for the future – Judeo-Christian biblical conception of time

2. Change of doctrine (Christianity + Greek philosophy) – self-critical

3. Personal (individual freedom) autonomy

4. The ongoing tension between liberty and equality

5. Political freedom (Augustine)

6. Toleration

7. Scientific and technological revolutions (God as Creator)

8. Economic freedom (evolved from Augustine → Aquinas →) – See Chapter 4

9. Constructive globalization

CHAPTER THREE

AMERICA AND THE SPIRITUAL QUEST OF MODERNITY

"God, who has given the world to men in common, has also given them reason to make use of it to the best advantage of life, and convenience. The Earth, and all that is therein, is given to men for the support and comfort of their being . . . it cannot be supposed He meant it should always remain common and uncultivated. He gave it to the use of the Industrious and Rational (and *Labor* was to be his *title* to it) not to the Fancy or Covetousness of the Quarrelsome and Contentious. . . . For it is *labor* indeed that *puts the difference of value on everything* . . . of the *products* of the earth useful to the life of man nine tenths are the effects of labor." – John Locke, *Second Treatise* (1690), Chapter Five (Of Property), sections 26, 27, 34, and 40.

Introduction

In this chapter we shall instantiate America as the modern exemplar of the Judeo-Christian heritage of spiritual capital. Toward that end, we present two theses in this chapter. The first thesis concerns the *logic of modernity*. What distinguishes modernity is the "technological project," the transformation of nature for human betterment (Descartes and Bacon) as opposed to fatalistic conformity. The technological project requires inner-directed individuals (St. Ignatius of Loyola's spiritual exercises, for example) and free market economies that maximize competition and innovation (David Hume and Adam Smith). Free market economies operate best with limited government (Montesquieu's commercial republic and Madison's *Federalist #10*). Limited government can only be maintained under the rule of law (Dicey, Fuller, Hayek, and Oakeshott). The rule of law can only be sustained if there is a larger cultural context that celebrates individual autonomy. Finally, individual autonomy presupposes a larger ontological claim about human freedom or free will that requires a theology. Moreover, personal autonomy avoids self-destruction and adds a spiritual content to the technological project itself when the responsible use of freedom leads to helping to fulfill God's plan by eliminating suffering and promoting freedom in others.

Technological Project → Free Market Economy → Limited Government → Rule of Law → Culture of Personal Autonomy → Personal God of the Judeo-Christian Heritage → Technological Project

Recognizing, pursuing, and sustaining autonomy are the spiritual quests of modernity and the technological project. The ultimate rationale for the technological project is not material comfort or consumer satisfaction, but the production of the means of accomplishment. *To discover that our greatest sense of fulfillment comes from freely imposing order on ourselves in order to impose a creative order on the world is perhaps the closest way of coming to know God.* Three considerations lead us to maintain that personal autonomy requires theological support. First, personal autonomy as we understand it presupposes free will. This amounts to saying that there is no naturalistic (and scientific) explanation of the ultimate truths about who we are. Second, we understand ourselves as historical beings, but history does not form a self-explanatory system. Our interpretation of the whole human drama depends on an intimately personal decision concerning the part we mean to play in it. In the end, this is a religious decision, not a scientific or scholarly one. Finally, sustaining our autonomy under trying circumstances requires spiritual stamina. Since it has been argued elsewhere (*The Enlightenment Project in the Analytic Conversation*), and we will expand upon it in the last chapter, that naturalism and scientism fail, theology in some important sense emerges as the only discipline that can provide ultimate comprehension.

The second thesis is the documented history of how settlers and immigrants to the United States brought this larger view to America, nourished it, and sustained it. There is a great deal of good literature on this, both classical work such as Tocqueville's *Democracy in America,* and to cite just two recent examples, Samuel P. Huntington's *Who Are We?,* and Ellis Sandoz's *Republicanism, Religion, and the Soul of America.* We will be largely summarizing the work of others in this part of the chapter.

The Logic of Modernity

The most important historical development in the last four hundred years has been the rise of the Technological Project (TP).[1] The TP, not the market, is the starting point for our narrative, because, although there have always been markets, it is only since the 16th century that markets have come to play such a dominant role in our lives. It is the presence of the TP that explains the centrality of markets.

The TP is the control of nature for human benefit. The TP (a) radically changed the way people in the West viewed the world and their relationship to the world, (b) led to fundamental changes in the major institutions of the West (economic, political,

---

1   The so-called industrial revolution is but an expression of the Technological Project. The more fundamental idea is the notion of transforming the world. See René Descartes, *Discourse on Method*; Francis Bacon, *Essays* (Amherst, N. Y. 1995) nos. 13, 16-17, and *The Great Instauration and New Atlantis,* ed. Jerry Weinberger (Arlington Heights, Ill. 1980).

legal, and social), (c) led to the expansion of the West and its domination of the non-Western world, and (d) led finally to globalization – the internationalization of Western institutions.

We make the following claims with regard to the TP:

a. It is an irreversible historical fact [protesters are forced to use technology in order to mount a protest against it, especially cell phones, the internet, and computers].

b. Abandonment of the TP would have catastrophic consequences for humanity and threaten its very existence.

c. To the extent that the TP creates environmental and other kinds of problems, we are now irrevocably committed to using future developments in the TP to address and hopefully solve those problems.

d. Those cultures which have most fully embraced the TP (including military technology) have come to dominate the world and to spread the TP. The spread has not been a matter of the powerful imposing on the weak; the weak have largely come to embrace the project on their own. The thorny issues of globalization would not have developed outside of the context of the technological project.

In the ancient and medieval world (and in much of the world today) people thought in terms of conformity to nature, not transforming nature for human benefit. In large part this reflected the fact that the earliest civilizations were agrarian, that agriculture requires in its early stages a calendar, and that the earliest calendars were based upon astronomy. This understandably fostered the mindset of believing that the physical world had a structure and meaning independent of human beings, that truth consisted in the apprehension of a structure independent of human beings, and that wisdom and success depended upon human beings conforming to the external structure of the world.

During the Renaissance all of that was to change. Starting with Copernicus, Western thinkers became aware of how much of what we understand reflects the human perspective (and so did the artists of the Renaissance). Copernicus, for example, maintained that despite appearances the sun does not rise and set, rather the earth turns on its axis. Starting with Copernicus and reinforced by the work of Galileo, Descartes, and Newton, Western thinkers came to recognize how much of science depended not on naïve observation of surface phenomena but on the construction of hypothetical *mathematical* models about hidden structure. Newton and Leibniz would both go on to invent the calculus. Meaning and structure (and in a word truth) were not to be found externally but in the internal models of the human mind. Wisdom and success were transformed from conformity to an external structure to bending or conforming the external physical world to human reason and imagination. The belief that human beings could understand and control the hidden structure of nature and that the hidden structure was conducive to human benefit was inspired, as we saw in the previous chapter, by Christianity! The medieval feudal-agrarian economy was not a central feature of Christianity but a particular historical context, one that was about to be transcended.

The medieval Aristotelian synthesis in which all of nature and humanity were linked in an inter-locking series of organic associations arranged in hierarchical order was rejected. Nature was no longer to be viewed as an organism but as a mechanism created by God. We as individuals inspired by an internally apprehended divine vision replicated God's creativity by transforming the world through good works including commerce and industry (not just charity). There was no collective good to be authoritatively apprehended in nature, only a collection of individually apprehended goods whose continuity and coherence were vouchsafed by God. The traditional Aristotelian view is still to be found among those who have turned environmentalism into a religion!

Among the first to proclaim the TP as a self-conscious undertaking were Francis Bacon,[2] when he proclaimed that "knowledge

---

2 Many scholars, for a variety of reasons, keep making the allegation that the early promoters of the logic of modernity and modernity itself are necessarily secular. This is a charge that continually gets rebutted. See for example Stephen McKnight, *The Religious Foundations of Francis Bacon's Thought* (2006).

is power," and René Descartes, French philosopher, mathemati-
cian, and physicist, who advocated that human beings make
themselves "the masters and possessors of nature." It is worth
noting that Descartes specifically singled out the importance of
advances in medical science for an age in which the normal
human life span was 36 years! It was also Descartes who in his
Discourse on Method advocated the development of inner-directed individuals (autonomy) cooperating to produce innovative
ideas (scientific and technical thinking) for understanding and
controlling natural processes. Finally, Descartes also recognized
how commercial republics like Holland in the 17th century were
peculiarly hospitable to these new developments.

The TP is fostered by an environment in which human beings
are given as much free reign as possible to use their imagination
(a) to think scientifically in the mathematical-modeling sense, and
(b) to develop new ways and products for humanity to control the
physical environment, to protect and heal the human body, and to
make life more comfortable and enjoyable. The economic institution most conducive to the TP was the free market economy
(FME): a system for the exchange of goods and services wherein
there is no central allocation of such goods and services. The
goods and services are privately owned (i.e., private property).
The FME fosters competition.

The market economy was not itself new. In fact, it could be
maintained that private property had always existed in historical
memory. The Church, moreover, had officially defended the
importance of private property. What was new was the recognition of how crucial private property and a free market economy
were to the TP. Why is that? Innovation cannot, by definition, be
planned. To the extent that property is privately owned and not
centrally controlled, and to the extent that a free market economy
is *competitive*, there is a greater possibility for innovation. In his
canonical work which marked the beginning of modern economic theory, Adam Smith argued in the *Wealth of Nations* (1776) that
a free market economy encouraged innovation. It was innovative

because the division of labor led to specialization and specialization led to innovation (labor-saving devices, etc.) as well as greater productivity. Smith's example of the manufacturing of pins explains how an assembly line of narrowly focused specialists is far more productive. Once we focus on one part of a process we are apt to invent labor-saving devices. Because it is the best vehicle for innovation, the free market economy is the best form of economic system for engaging in the TP. Finally, the historical-empirical argument for the advantages of a free market economy is the 1989 implosion of the Soviet Union. Almost everywhere it is now admitted that a free market economy is the most efficient method for engaging in the technological project.

While private property had always existed, governments from time immemorial had regulated and controlled it in varying degrees to advance their own purposes and not for the TP. To get the maximum advantage out of a market economy it needs to be as free as possible to foster innovation. Government or the State can play a useful but limited function by providing a legal system for protecting the rights of individuals, especially private property, for enforcing contracts, and for dispute resolution. In order for a free market economy to function it requires a limited government (LG) known as a commercial republic. The government provides the legal context for maintaining law and order and for enforcing contracts. It requires as well that the government which performs this service understand that it should not interfere with the competitive and innovative process of the market. The government exists to protect the rights of individuals who pursue their own individual interests (*civil association*). It does not exist to further a collective good (*enterprise association*) or to serve the bureaucracy or to serve a particular interest group. This is the sense in which the government is limited or subordinate to the requirements of commerce. Instead of employing slogans like the "night watchman state" or the "minimal" state, it is more insightful to recognize that state action is best when restricted to serving the interests of a market economy within the technological project. Needless to add, Christianity had provided a tradition for limiting the government and the Church had steadfastly maintained the inviolability of private property – including and especially its own!

This form of government is called a *Republic*. It is a government of laws and not of men. A republic is designed to protect the rights of individuals, not the privileges of a majority or a minority. It has a Constitution which specifies those rights. Since there is no collective good, there is a common good. The common good consists of the conditions (e.g., rule of law, toleration) within which individuals pursue their self-interest.

A Republic is not a democracy, for a democracy involves majority rule and not constitutional rule. From Plato and Aristotle right through the eighteenth-century Founding, democracy was rejected as mob rule. Democracy technically means majority rule, and in practice becomes a system of political economy in which the bottom 51 percent progressively loot the wealth and productivity of the top 49 percent.

Democracy was understood by the Founders as part of a system of checks and balances[3] that prevents one interest from imposing its will upon others. Democracy, as Madison made clear in *Federalist # 10*, is a negative device for blocking one powerful interest group from imposing its will on others. Democracy was never intended as a positive device for articulating a suspect common good. It was during the nineteenth century in Europe that democracy as majority rule was posited as the will of the people. That is when Tocqueville and Mill came to view democracy as a threat, as the tyranny of the majority.[4] It evolved into the formal notion that what is right is what the majority decides, or that the common good is what the majority decides it is on a given occasion.

3   Sen's paradox (1970) presents a more precise formulation of why democracy is a negative device rather than a positive one. Marxists have always been rightly contemptuous of democratic socialism because shifting majorities literally make even the façade of economic planning impossible.
4   Public choice economics in the work of James Buchanan and others helps to explain the structure of that degeneration.

In the post-Renaissance and Reformation period, Protestants especially[5] saw an important connection between politics and economics. The desire for political equality was not the desire to exercise power for power's sake or to remake society. On the contrary, Protestants were largely focused on protecting the private sphere and the spiritual dimension from political corruption. The connection between politics and economics derived from the fact that government controlled large parts of the economy (granting of privileges such as monopolies, sinecures, land grants, etc.). Political equality implied economic equality in the sense that all possessed the liberty to pursue God's work in this world, not an equal distribution of the spoils.

Part of the meaning of political equality was equality before the law, and equality before the law meant appeal to the rule of law and not the whim of political leaders. One of the institutional ways in which government is limited is through the rule of law. *Behind the notion of the rule of law lies the historical notion that not all law is just law – that there is a higher law in terms of which ordinary law could be challenged.* Going back to the classical Greeks, a distinction was made between positive or man-made law and the law of nature – the latter being understood as normative. Aristotle explained natural law in terms of a purely naturalistic and teleological conception of the universe – everything has a purpose and the entire set of all purposes forms a natural hierarchy. Throughout the medieval and early modern period Christianity had adopted and advocated the tradition of natural law. Christians identified natural law ultimately with the will of God. Aquinas sought to harmonize Christianity with Aristotle. Aquinas posited a hierarchy of divine law, biblical law, natural law, and positive law. Positive or man-made law was to be judged in terms of its conformity to the natural law. Even the meaning of positive law was clarified by appeal to natural law. The latter was accessible through reason supplemented by bibli-

---

5   For the moment, the discussion of Christianity will focus on Protestantism; later we shall explain how Catholicism came to share some of these features.

cal law. Crucial to the development of the rule of law in England was the theologian Richard Hooker, who adapted Thomistic notions of natural law to the Church of England and influenced John Locke, who quotes him extensively in the *Second Treatise*.

The demand for equality before the law was an expression of the notion of Christian liberty. In rejecting a hierarchical conception of the world, Protestants could accept that the political realm was no longer subordinate to the religious realm. But, at the same time, the political realm had to respect the traditional spiritual realm of Christianity. That realm as understood in Protestant terms meant the opportunity to do God's work by transforming the world economically. Equality before the law came to mean that there should be no legal barriers to economic activity that did not apply equally to everyone. Placing legal barriers in the economic realm was tantamount to thwarting God's plan!

The rule of law (RL) has evolved jurisprudentially into meaning a legal system that *constrains government*.[6] Typically in

6   See F.H.A. Hayek, *Law, Legislation, and Liberty* (London: Taylor & Francis, 1982) and *The Road to Serfdom* (Chicago: University of Chicago Press, 1994), Chapter Six "Planning and the Rule of Law"; M. Oakeshott, "The Rule of Law," in *On History and Other Essays* (1983), pp. 119-164; Supplement (*On Human Conduct*, pp. 119, 139, 181, 153-58 [mentions Fuller], 234–35, 286, and 315) 56pp. Free economic activity, effective economic competition and free markets unfettered by monopolies are, in Oakeshott's words, "not something that springs up of its own accord," but are "the creature of law." They are CREATED by the systematic rule of law. Economic competition can only exist, Oakeshott maintains, by virtue of a legal system "which promotes it." This underscores the fact that for Oakeshott "a connection is drawn between the rule of law and a free society" as a whole. This explicit language of promotion, creation, connection, suggests some causal relation between rule of law and economic and general freedom. From the vantage point of the economist, it could be argued that one direct PURPOSE of the rule of law is to maximize economic utility. However, this of course directly conflicts with Oakeshott's famous insistence that the rule of law is a mode of ethical association in terms of the recognition of the authority of known, NON-INSTRUMENTAL laws. Such ethical association are fundamentally distinguished by Oakeshott from purposive or enterprise associations. As Oakeshott points out in his *Rule of Law*, many apologists of the rule of law, "recognizing the inconsistency of attributing the virtue of a non-instrumental mode of association to its propensity to produce, promote or encourage" a substantive

practice the powers of government are divided among separate branches, with an independent judiciary. Due process and the equal protection of the law protects the rights of individuals by constitutional means. It is a system of rules designed to allow individuals to pursue their self-defined interests without interfering with that same pursuit on the part of others. *The rule of law provides the rules of the game without determining the outcome of the game.* As elaborated by Michael Oakeshott, the rule of law exists only in a modern state that is a civil association, that is, one in

outcome, have insisted that the Rule of Law's specific virtue is precisely its promotion of the outcome of either peace, order, economic efficiency or more prominently freedom. But such outcomes, Oakeshott maintains, are not the consequences of an association of legal persona, but instead are INHERENT IN ITS CHARACTER, thus characterized by it. Given these subtle differences, the questions arise: what precisely is the difference, especially in terms of outcome, between an inherent substantive condition and one resulting from a purposive action? Most importantly in this context what difference would these differences, if any, make to economists? How would Oakeshott's view of the relation between the legal non-instrumental mode of association and freedom affect the economists understanding of the relation between law and economic systems? Would it make a difference to economics whether a free market system is INHERENT IN THE CHARACTER of an association of legal persona, or whether it is the explicit purpose of a legal system? Does it matter to various economic theories to be aware of Oakeshottean distinctions, or are they irrelevant? That to me is one of the most interesting points implicitly raised by Oakeshott. The beginning, only the beginning, of an answer would be that all talk about the *purpose* of law is unconfirmable and irresolvable metaphysical mischief. The law and economics defenders (e.g., Posner) do not have to provide additional arguments for their contention; their position is inherent in the very idea of the rule of law. Another way of putting this is that the familiar claim that there is no government that respects individual freedom unless there is first a free market should be rendered as: free markets only exist where there is a government that respects individual freedom. The notion that authoritarian societies exhibit free markets is a mistake; sometimes such societies are characterized as capitalist (Marxist concept), but no society where one group can arbitrarily and "legally" exclude others from the market can be said to be a free market society.

It is a misleading caricature in law and economics; to say that free market economic objectives are promoted by the rule of law as a consequence, is not to say that a specific consequence is the objective or purpose of the law.

Oakeshott notes that no society perfectly instantiates the rule of law. Moreover, the rule of law is threatened by ever-increasing government bureaucracies, war, and the anti-individual.

which there is no collective good, only the good of its individual members. The laws prescribe conditions to be observed by individuals who pursue their own purposes, alone or with others. The laws are neutral or indifferent with regard to whether the purposes are achieved. Once the law is construed as an instrument for achieving particular economic or political objectives, the rule of law is violated or disappears. Affirmative action as quotas is a preeminent example of the violation of the rule of law.

All of the above institutions both reflect a certain kind of culture and promote that kind of culture. There is an important connection between spiritual capital and autonomy. "Purpose refers to a person's belief that life has meaning. Autonomy refers to a person's belief that it is in his power to fulfill that meaning through his own acts . . . creativity ultimately comes down to small, solitary acts in which an individual conceives of something new and gives it a try, without knowing for sure how it will turn out. Streams of accomplishment are more common and more extensive in cultures where doing new things and acting autonomously are encouraged than in cultures that disapprove."[7]

In order for a government to remain limited and not become either authoritarian or totalitarian or subject to mob-rule (i.e., democracy), it is necessary that the citizens of that government be special kinds of people. They must be autonomous people. Autonomous people are those who rule themselves (i.e., they impose order on their lives through self-discipline in order to achieve goals that they have set for themselves).

It is important to avoid misinterpretations and misrepresentations of a culture of personal autonomy. A culture of personal autonomy is not a culture of self-indulgence. Merely to acquiesce in bodily and emotional impulses is not autonomy but a form of slavery – becoming a slave to one's passions. In order to fulfill God's plan, human beings need to know how to control

7   Murray, pp. 394–99.

themselves. Moreover, autonomous beings do not impose their will on others. To define oneself in such a way as merely to defy others or to require that others be your victim is to define oneself in terms of others – the opposite of autonomy. Hence, to act autonomously is to presume that the ultimate ends of each individual are consistent with the ultimate ends of all other individuals. The will of God no longer has its locus in nature outside of human effort. Rather the will of God is discerned inwardly through self-discipline. We imitate God by freeing our will of all influences except the recognition of its freedom, by freely choosing to create a world or to help in creating a world in which the ultimate interests of all coalesce, in which the ultimate interest of each individual is to express its freedom so understood. The so-called Protestant work ethic promoted the notions of (a) the inner-directed individual, (b) an emphasis on achievement through work, (c) equality before the law, and (d) differentiation based on achievement.

It is the combination of the TP, the FME, and autonomy that account for the appearance of a new persona, the entrepreneur. In the sixteenth century we find the first use of the term entrepreneur, from the French verb *entreprendre* – to undertake something. The entrepreneur discovers (Israel Kirzner view) or imagines (Schumpeter view) new ways of combining resources to create new products or new methods of production. The entrepreneur engages in what Joseph Schumpeter was to call creative-destruction.

Autonomous people are inner-directed and therefore capable of participating in the TP in a creative and constructive way. In fact, *the ultimate purpose of the TP is not simply to create wealth but to allow autonomous people to express their freedom and how such freedom reflects God's will*. Wealth is a means to achievement and freedom, not an end in itself. It is in this sense that the TP is now to be understood as the spiritual quest of modernity. The ultimate rationale for the technological project is not consumer satisfaction but the production of the means of accomplishment. Our greatest fulfillment comes from freely imposing order on ourselves in order to impose a creative order on the world. We have now come full circle. We started with the TP and now we have explained that even the TP is an expression of spiritual capital.

The Judeo-Christian roots of autonomy are evident: it is the culmination of the Christian doctrine of free will and responsibility transposed to the civil sphere. Many social scientists will offer some resistance at this point. Those committed to scientism (or extreme versions of positivism) may concede that religious belief has in fact played a significant role in affecting market behavior and social institutions in the past and present, but they may also think that it "ought" not to have this influence in the future. Our argument, on the contrary, is that (a) the spiritual dimension is a "necessary" condition for the continued vitality of free societies; (b) any form of scientism is intellectually deficient, and (c) scientism cannot generate an adequate account of ethical principles.

Autonomous people want to run their own lives, and they do not want the government or any other institution to control them. They are jealous of their liberties and want the government to be restricted to its proper spheres. They are focused on taking care of themselves and not looking for others to take care of them. The abuse of democratic procedure requires the political and legal machinery of checks and balances. Political machinery ultimately depends on the larger cultural context. We are, therefore, brought back to the need for a culture that preserves something like the importance of individuality.

Autonomous people want recognition of their autonomy. This recognition can only come from other autonomous people who understand what self-discipline requires. Autonomous people seek to promote autonomy in others in order to encourage this recognition. They believe in helping others. But promoting the autonomy of others does not mean redistribution; it means equality of opportunity, not equality of result; it means holding everyone accountable, not condescension; it means when necessary teaching others how to fish, not giving them a fish.

Autonomy is not zero-sum. The ultimate self-interest of autonomous people is never in conflict with the ultimate self-interest of others.

In the ancient and medieval world there was no poverty problem! Almost everyone was poor and poverty was considered the natural and unavoidable condition of the human race. As a result of the TP, we can now contemplate a world of such abundance that no one will be poor in the absolute sense, a world marked by ever increasing growth and opportunity.

For us, then, poverty is a problem to be solved. Why do we find poverty both domestically and abroad? The absence of autonomy explains the existence of dysfunctional people, including the poor, in free societies. The politically correct diagnosis for the existence of dysfunctional people, and we might add every conceivable social problem, is the lack of resources. The default remedy, given the politically correct diagnosis, is some form of redistribution. But if we[8] are right, the existence of these dysfunctional people and a whole host of social problems is the presence of people who have not yet developed a sense of personal autonomy. In a world of near-universal grinding poverty and little hope of extrication, we can understand the need for social cohesion and conformity; in such a world one can understand why people are risk-averse and focused on the fear of failure. We think this is true both domestically and internationally.

What are the global implications of the foregoing? A national government is obliged to serve the market economy not only at home but abroad. Modern commerce creates wealth through the TP, not by stealing it from our neighbors. As Hume, Smith, Constant, and Kant pointed out, a domestic market leads to constructive competition and specialization so an international market will do so as well.

One of the consequences, therefore, of modern commerce is the potential end of war, what Kant referred to as perpetual

8   This explanation is borrowed from Michael Oakeshott's discussion of autonomy in the "Masses in Representative Democracy," where he identifies the dysfunctional as anti-individuals.

peace.[9] As Kant went on to argue, commercial republics do not go to war with each other. This hypothesis has enormous empirical support. It has been argued that in the last two hundred years since Kant wrote *Perpetual Peace*, there have been no major wars where all of the combatants on both sides have been commercial republics. This is also sometimes called the "McDonald effect," since no two countries where McDonald's fast food is available go to war with each other. If the entire world consisted of commercial republics, there would be no war and no need for a world government or even a world court; all contractual disputes could be resolved through national or regional jurisdictional courts. A world court is unnecessary; if all countries are committed to the rule of law, and if all contracts specify where disputes are to be resolved, a world court would be a needless duplication. The current UN would not be what Kant had in mind: most of the countries that belong are not commercial republics (France included – it remains mercantilist); the Security Council has veto-power members at present who are opposed to the logic of modernity. A similar problem haunts the EU, an organization seemingly committed to mercantilism and to French cultural hegemony.

This leads to the following tension and paradox: domestically the government is to maintain a low profile and a fairly passive supporting role for commerce, but in the international context the government is to promote actively the entire panoply of TP, FME, LG, and RL. To intervene in foreign affairs to bring about this result is incumbent upon free governments. It is no use pretending that the implications could be otherwise.

The following qualifications need to be kept in mind:
(a) When and how to intervene requires judgment and a weigh ing of costs and benefits. This debate will always be subject to argument.

---

9   Fukuyama, *The End of History and the Last Man* (New York: Free Press, 1992) (Kojève's interpretation of Hegel inspired Fukuyama); see also Hegel's discussion of Adam Smith in *The Philosophy of Right*.

(b) Arguments about what to introduce or cultivate first (mar kets or limited government or rule of law) fail to comprehend that this is a package deal. not a sequential relation ship.

(c) Politically correct mantras about respecting other cultures ignore the extent to which cultural change is part of the package. All cultures undergo change over time.

(d) Isolationism (both military and economic) will not work except as escapism because

(i) as long as some countries resist Kant's claims in *Perpetual Peace*, defending the country against aggression has to be done anyway; and

(ii) to the extent that other countries or non-state entities perceive themselves as enterprise associations (e.g., some versions of Islam, various forms of nationalism such as Russia, China, etc.) they will be and act as adversaries to free societies.

(e) There are those who reject the paradox because they are themselves in an adversarial position to the logic of modernity and to the U.S. as its greatest exemplar.

(f) Recent debates about "American Exceptionalism" are disguised debates about the legitimacy of countries like the U.S. founded on the logic of modernity.

The greatest obstacle to globalization is the resistance to cultural change, specifically resistance to the notion of personal autonomy. Some will argue that this amounts to western cultural hegemony. Our response would be, first, that autonomy is a fundamental truth about human nature and that its prevalence in the West is the result of the Judeo-Christian heritage. Second, those non-Westerners who have experienced and embraced personal autonomy recognize that it is an irreversible transformation of the self, not one choice among many; in fact, the notion of choosing an identity only makes sense if we have the capacity for autonomy. Third, cultures are not rigid structures but historical artifacts that change over time, most especially when confronted with alternative cultures. Finally, as V.S. Naipaul has put it, the "idea of the pursuit of happiness . . . is an elastic idea; it fits all men. It implies a certain kind of society, a certain kind of awakened spirit. We don't imagine my father's parents would have been able to understand the idea. So much is contained in it: the idea of the individual, responsibility, choice, the life of the intellect, the idea of vocation and perfectibility and achievement. It is an immense human idea. It cannot be reduced to a fixed system. It cannot generate fanaticism. But it is known to exist; and because of that, other more rigid systems in the end are blown away."[10] One does not impose personal autonomy, and that is the secret of its power.

America as Exceptional Exemplar of the Logic of Modernity

America is the best and clearest exemplar of the logic of modernity. No culture is more committed to the Technological Project, and no country receives more Nobel Prizes for advances in the sciences than the United States. The United States remains the leading exemplar of the idea of free markets, and a large part of its diplomacy consists in establishing free trade agreements. This is also a striking example of the Kantian plan for perpetual peace. No country espouses limited government more than the United States, and the recent (2010) activity of the Tea Party confirms the fact that no culture is more committed to limited government. The United States is not only the clearest example of a country committed to the rule of law, but most global commercial contracts contain a clause referencing U.S. courts as the locus of adjudication in case of disputes. Whatever side one takes on Guantanamo refugees, it is hard to imagine another country where the status of their legal rights would be debated at all. Moreover, the U.S. uses its influence with the WTO and the World Bank to focus loans on countries attempting to implement the rule of law. Finally, America is the example *par excellence* of

10 The Manhattan Institute for Policy Research, The 1990 Wriston Lecture, *Our Universal Civilization*, V. S. Naipaul, October 30, 1990, New York City.

rugged individualism, and its Hollywood westerns are popular throughout the world because of its proclamation of that message. "Cowboy Capitalism" may be an expression of derision to many, but no one would apply it to any country other than the U.S.

Michel Guillaume Jean de Crèvecœur was born in France in 1735, emigrated to North America in 1755, and became an American citizen in 1770, taking the name John Hector St. John. Following the American Revolution, he published in 1782 *Letters from an American Farmer*. He was the first writer to describe for Europeans what it was to be an American, enunciating the American Dream and characterizing American society in terms of autonomy and equal opportunity.

> What then is the American, this new man? He is either an European, or the descendant of an European, hence that strange mixture of blood, which you will find in no other country. I could point out to you a family whose grandfather was an Englishman, whose wife was Dutch, whose son married a French woman, and whose present four sons have now four wives of different nations. *He* is an American, who leaving behind him all his ancient prejudices and manners, receives new ones from the new mode of life he has embraced, the new government he obeys, and the new rank he holds. He becomes an American by being received in the broad lap of our great *Alma Mater*. Here individuals of all nations are melted into a new race of men, whose labours and posterity will one day cause great changes in the world. Americans are the western pilgrims, who are carrying along with them that great mass of arts, sciences, vigour, and industry which began long since in the east; they will finish the great circle. The Americans were once scattered all over Europe; here they are incorporated into one of the finest systems of population which has ever appeared, and which will hereafter become distinct by the power of the different climates they inhabit. The American ought therefore to love this country much better than that wherein either he or his forefathers were born. Here the rewards of his industry follow with equal steps the progress of his labour; his labour is founded on the basis of nature, *self-interest*; can it want a

stronger allurement? Wives and children, who before in vain demanded of him a morsel of bread, now, fat and frolicsome, gladly help their father to clear those fields whence exuberant crops are to arise to feed and to clothe them all; without any part being claimed, either by a despotic prince, a rich abbot, or a mighty lord . . . religion demands but little of *him*; a small voluntary salary to the minister, and gratitude to God; can he refuse these? The American is a new man, who acts upon new principles; he must therefore entertain new ideas, and form new opinions. From involuntary idleness, servile dependence, penury, and useless labour, he has passed to toils of a very different nature, rewarded by ample subsistence. – This is an American.

To the extent that the logic of modernity is rooted in Judeo-Christian spiritual capital, America is unique in preserving that connection. Americans continue to identify themselves overwhelmingly with the Judeo-Christian spiritual heritage, long after it has disappeared as the cultural foundation of the EU (Western Europe). That is why most Americans subscribe to the Lockean Liberty narrative (to be discussed in a later chapter), not the equality narrative that now dominates Europe; it is why America can combine a secular civil association with a religious culture instead of the Muslim belief in an enterprise theocracy; it is why America celebrates autonomy instead of the Asian belief in social conformity.

Unlike the French who mostly came to the New World for commercial activity, e.g., fur trade, and unlike the Spanish who may have come for "Gold, Glory, and God" but also for the extension of serfdom, the English *settlers* came to America to start a new life. They analogized themselves in Biblical terms to Moses leading the Jews out of the desert and into the Promised Land. In *The Mayflower Compact* (1620), they proclaimed "In the name of God, Amen . . . having undertaken, for the glory of God, and the advancement of the Christian faith . . . a voyage to plant the first colony." In 1630, John Winthrop spoke of New England as "a City upon a Hill, the eyes of all people are upon us." In short, many of the early settlers saw themselves as a Chosen

People. This is reiterated by Abraham Lincoln who in planning the Emancipation Proclamation saw the U.S. as "the last best hope on earth."[11] It is echoed as well in President Ronald Reagan's 1989 *Farewell Address* when he reiterated the commitment to the "shining city upon a hill."[12] There is a clear connection between monotheism and proselytism, for only those who believe in one true God seek to convert others; and there is a secondary connection with Christianity for what "Christianity offered the world was monotheism stripped of ethnic encumbrances."[13]

Early American settlers gave it a specifically Anglo-Protestant identity. As Samuel Huntington has argued, American identity has had two primary components: culture and creed. The creed is a set of universal principles articulated in our founding documents: liberty, equality, democracy, constitutionalism, limited government, and private property. Our culture is Anglo-Protestant, specifically dissenting Protestantism. Moreover, the creed is itself the product of "English traditions, dissenting Protestantism, and Enlightenment ideas of the eighteenth-century settlers."[14]

One way of characterizing the early U.S. is to say that it inherited the logic of modernity and all of its institutions (the technological project [Bacon], economic [Smith], political [Locke], and legal [common law]) from Great Britain. What distinguished the U.S. from England were three crucial things: (a) the lack of a feudal class structure which dominated Great Britain down into the twentieth century, (b) an extensive virgin territory for applying it, and most especially (c) the opportunity for a multitude of dissenting Protestant sects, Catholics, and Jews to engage the new world with a religious fervor largely absent from the feudalistic Church of England. It is important to

---

11 Abraham Lincoln, *Annual Message to Congress*, December 1, 1862.
12 www.ronaldreagan.com/sp_21.html (November 4, 2009).
13 Rodney Stark, *Cities of God* (New York: Harper-Collins, 2006), p. 7.
14 Samuel P. Huntington, *Who Are WE?* (New York: Simon & Schuster, 2005), pp. 339–40.

remember how many of the original settlers were from dissenting Protestant sects such as the Puritans and Quakers.

This early influence can be seen in the sermons preached
during the American War of Independence, the Declaration of
Independence, and throughout the rest of U.S. history.[15] Here is
a brief sampling.

 * *The Declaration of Independence* asserts that "All men . . . are
endowed by their Creator with certain unalienable Rights, that
among these are Life, Liberty and the pursuit of happiness." The
last sentence asserts "a firm reliance on divine Providence."

 * The Liberty Bell contains a verse from the *Torah*: "Proclaim
liberty throughout the land."[16]

 * George Washington's 1790 letter to the Hebrew
Congregation at Newport: "May the children of the stock of
Abraham who dwell in this land continue to merit and enjoy the
good will of the other inhabitants - while everyone shall sit in
safety under his own vine and fig tree and there shall be none to
make him afraid. May the father of all mercies scatter light, and
not darkness, upon our paths, and make us all in our several
vocations useful here, and in His own due time and way ever-
lastingly happy."

 * John Adams, "Statesmen may plan and speculate for liberty, but it is Religion and Morality alone which can establish the
Principles upon which Freedom can securely stand."

 * In his classic *Democracy in America* (1840), Tocqueville identified America's unique religious heritage derived primarily
from the Puritans, the importance of the Hebrew Bible, and the
transposed belief that America was a chosen nation whose
founding gave Americans a sense of moral mission. Most especially, Tocqueville observed that the Biblical outlook gave
America a moral dimension which the Old World lacked. "I have
said enough to put the character of Anglo-American civilization

---

15   See John A. Howard, *Christianity: Lifeblood of America's Free Society* (Summit
     Press, 2007).
16   See the works of prominent Jewish author and journalist Dennis Prager.

in its true light. It is the result (and this should be constantly kept in mind) of two distinct elements, which in other places have been in frequent disagreement, but which the Americans have succeeded in incorporating to some extent one with the other and combining admirably. I allude to the spirit of religion and the spirit of liberty.[17]

* Lincoln's Gettysburg Address concludes with: "We here highly resolve . . . that this nation, under God, shall have a new birth of freedom – and that government of the people, by the people, for the people, shall not perish from the earth."

* In 1952 President-elect Dwight Eisenhower acknowledged that the "Judeo-Christian concept" is the "deeply religious faith" on which "our sense of government . . . is founded."

* "Under God" was added to the Pledge of Allegiance in 1954.

* The national motto (since 1956) which appears on U.S. currency is "In God we trust."

* Presidents take the oath of office on an Old and New Testament Bible.

America exemplifies the logic of modernity *par excellence*. That is why there is such a thing as the American Dream. In his book *Epic of America*, James Truslow Adams described it as follows:

> The American Dream is that dream of a land in which life should be better and richer and fuller for every man, with opportunity for each according to ability or achievement. It is a difficult dream for the European upper classes to interpret adequately, also too many of us ourselves have grown weary and mistrustful of it. It is not a dream of motor cars and high wages merely, but a dream of social order in which each man and each woman shall be able to attain to the fullest stature of which they are innately capable, and be recognized by others for what they are, regardless of the fortuitous circumstances of birth or position. . . . The American Dream . . . has lured tens of millions of all nations to our

17   Alexis de Tocqueville, *Democracy in America*, Chapter Two.

shores in the past century has not been a dream of material plenty, though that has doubtlessly counted heavily. It has been a dream of being able to grow to fullest development as a man and woman, unhampered by the barriers which had slowly been erected in the older civilizations, unrepressed by social orders which had developed for the benefit of classes rather than for the simple human being of any and every class. "

There is something special about American patriotism. Patriotism is love of one's country. This can take many forms. Nationalism is a form of patriotism in which the political entity is identified with a particular ethnic group. Not all forms of patriotism are nationalistic. Jingoism is another but extreme form of patriotism usually involving advocacy of the use of force against another country.

American patriotism is not nationalistic. Quite the contrary, the U.S. is a country of immigrants (quite literally everyone including so-called native Americans had ancestors who came from abroad) and accepts immigrants from everywhere. American culture is identified with a creed or set of ideas, not a place or an historically distinct people and certainly not a particular religious sect. Americans do not believe that they are unique – on the contrary, they believe that the American experiment and way of life can flourish among all peoples. Nor are Americans jingoistic; when the U.S. goes to war it is to allow other countries to be free and not to make them part of an American Empire. Recall post-war Germany and Japan. America does not seek hegemony. As Charles Krauthammer has put it, "We are the only Great Power in history who, upon arriving on a foreign shore, first asks the question 'What's the exit strategy?'"[18] The history of the world in the twentieth century is the history of how

18 Dr. Charles Krauthammer, "American Exceptionalism in the Age of Obama," Teaching Freedom, Fund for American Studies, www.tfas.org/Page.aspx?pid=2097. John Stuart Mill saw England as having a similar role in the nineteenth century. See his essay, *A Few Words on Non-Intervention*:

"There is a country in Europe, equal to the greatest in extent of dominion, far exceeding any other in wealth, and in the power that wealth bestows, the

America was primarily responsible for extending economic and political freedom throughout the world.

declared principle of whose foreign policy is, to let other nations alone. No country apprehends or affects to apprehend from it any aggressive designs. Power, from of old, is wont to encroach upon the weak, and to quarrel for ascendancy with those who are as strong as itself. Not so this nation. It will hold its own, it will not submit to encroachment, but if other nations do not meddle with it, it will not meddle with them. Any attempt it makes to exert influence over them, even by persuasion, is rather in the service of others, than of itself: to mediate in the quarrels which break out between foreign States, to arrest obstinate civil wars, to reconcile belligerents, to intercede for mild treatment of the vanquished, or finally, to procure the abandonment of some national crime and scandal to humanity, such as the slave-trade. Not only does this nation desire no benefit to itself at the expense of other, it desires none in which all others do not freely participate. It makes no treaties stipulating for separate commercial advantages. If the aggressions of barbarians force it to successful war, and its victorious arms put it in a position to command liberty of trade, whatever it demands for itself it demands for all mankind. The cost of the war is its own; the fruits it shares in fraternal equality with the whole human race. Its own ports and commerce are free as the air and the sky; all its neighbors have full liberty to resort to it, paying either no duties, or, if any, generally a mere equivalent for what is paid by its own citizens; nor does it concern itself though they, on their part, keep all to themselves, and persist in the most jealous and narrow-minded exclusion of its merchants and goods. A nation adopting this policy is a novelty in the world; so much so it would appear that many are unable to believe it when they see it. By one of the practical paradoxes which often meet us in human affairs, it is this nation which finds itself, in respect of its foreign policy, held up to obloquy as the type of egoism and selfishness; as a nation which thinks of nothing but of out-witting and out-generalling its neighbors. An enemy, or a self-fancied rival who had been distanced in the race, might be conceived to give vent to such an accusation in a moment of ill-temper. But that it should be accepted by lookers-on, and should pass into a popular doctrine, is enough to surprise even those who have best sounded the depths of human prejudice. Such, however, is the estimate of the foreign policy of England most widely current on the Continent. Let us not flatter ourselves that it is merely the dishonest pretence of enemies, or of those who have their own purposes to serve by exciting odium against us, a class including all the Protectionist writers, and the mouthpieces of all the despots and of the Papacy. The more blameless and laudable our policy might be, the more certainly we might count on its being misrepresented and railed at by those whom they can influence, but is held with all the tenacity of a prejudice, by innumerable persons free from interested bias. So strong a hold has it on their minds, that when an Englishman attempts to remove it, all their habitual politeness does not enable them to disguise their utter unbelief in his disclaimer. They are finally persuaded that no word is said, nor act done, by English statesmen in reference to foreign affairs, which has not for its motive principle some peculiarly English interest. Any profession of the contrary appears to them too ludicrously transparent an attempt to impose upon them. Those most friendly to us think they make a great concession in admitting that the fault may possibly be

Failure and Success of Catholicism in the New World

If one were to return to the sixteenth century and raise the question whether North America or South America would be

less with the English people, than with the English Government and aristocracy. We do not even receive credit from them for following our own interest with a straightforward recognition of honesty as the best policy. They believe that we have always other objects than those we avow; and the most far-fetched and implausible suggestion of a selfish purpose appears to them better entitled to credence than anything so utterly incredible as our disinterestedness. Thus, to give one instance among many, when we taxed ourselves twenty millions (a prodigious sum in their estimation) to get rid of negro slavery, and, for the same object, periled, as everybody thought, destroyed as many thought, the very existence of our West Indian colonies, it was, and still is, believed that our fine professions were but to delude the world, and that by this self-sacrificing behavior we were endeavoring to gain some hidden object, which could neither be conceived nor described, in the way of pulling down other nations. The fox who had lost his tail had an intelligible interest in persuading his neighbors to rid themselves of theirs: but we, it is thought by our neighbors, cut off our own magnificent brush, the largest and finest of all, in hopes of reaping some inexplicable advantage from inducing others to do the same. It is foolish attempting to despise all this - persuading ourselves that it is not our fault, and that those who disbelieve us would not believe though one should rise from the dead. Nations, like individuals, ought to suspect some fault in themselves when they find they are generally worse thought of than they think they deserve; and they may well know that they are somehow in fault when almost everybody but themselves thinks them crafty and hypocritical. It is not solely because England has been more successful than other nations in gaining what they are all aiming at, that they think she must be following after it with a more ceaseless and a more undivided chase. This indeed is a powerful predisposing cause, inclining and preparing them for the belief. It is a natural supposition that those who win the prize have striven for it; that superior success must be the fruit of more unremitting endeavor; and where there is an obvious abstinence from the ordinary arts employed for distancing competitors, and they are distanced nevertheless, people are fond of believing that the means employed must have been arts still more subtle and profound. This preconception makes them look out in all quarters for indications to prop up the selfish explanation of our conduct. If our ordinary course of action does not favor this interpretation, they watch for exceptions to our ordinary course, and regard these as the real index to the purposes within. They moreover accept literally all the habitual expressions by which we represent ourselves as worse than we are; expressions often heard from English statesmen, next to never from those of any other country - partly because Englishmen, beyond all the rest of the human race, are so shy of professing virtues that they will even profess vices instead; and partly because almost all English statesmen, while careless to a degree which no foreigner can credit, respecting the impression they produce on foreigners, commit the obtuse blunder of supposing that low objects are the more prosperous, the obvious answer then would be South America because of climate, natural resources, indigenous population, etc. That has obviously not been the case. Much scholarly attention has been given to the question of why Latin America has lagged in economic development. Obviously there are many factors to take into account, but we are especially interested in this question because of our claim that Christianity is the driving force behind the logic of modernity.

Clearly, Latin America is a Christian continent. If so, then why did it not fully embrace the logic of modernity? The answer at one level is that Latin America was settled by Spanish Catholics whereas North America was settled primarily by English Protestants. At a deeper level, it was not the Catholic dimension that was crucial but the Spanish dimension. What Spain exported to the New World was agrarian feudalism and not the logic of modernity. "The British colonies were founded on production, the Spanish colonies on extraction . . . emigrants from Britain . . . did not come in search of feudal estates or to mine gold and silver. Most of them came because of high wages prevailing in the colonies and the extraordinary opportunities to obtain fertile farmland or to set up a workshop or store."[19]

Moreover, the Catholic Church of the Counter-Reformation (last half of the sixteenth century and the first half of the seventeenth century) was a reactionary movement in the sense of trying to reestablish an enterprise association jointly ruled by the

only ones to which the minds of their non-aristocratic fellow-countrymen are amenable, and that it is always expedient, if not necessary, to place those objects in the foremost rank. All, therefore, who either speak or act in the name of England, are bound by the strongest obligations, both of prudence and of duty, to avoid giving either of these handles for misconstruction: to put a severe restraint upon the mania of professing to act from meaner motives than those by which we are really actuated, and to beware of perversely or capriciously singling out some particular instance in which to act on a worse principle than that by which we are ordinarily guided. Both these salutary cautions our practical statesmen are, at the present time, flagrantly disregarding. We are now in one of those critical moments . . ."

19 Rodney Stark, *The Victory of Reason: How Christianity Led to Freedom, Capitalism, and Western Success* (New York: Random House, 2005), pp. 212, 214.

State and Church. In return for making Catholicism the official state-supported religion, the Church acquiesced in monarchical tyranny. Hence, "it was not Catholicism but tyranny that imped-ed capitalism in France and Spain,"[20] and we would add Italy and Portugal. As a consequence, the Church in Latin America remained committed to a feudal-hierarchical society both in its own structure and in its view of civil society. "Spanish colonists in Latin America inherited a repressive and unproductive feu-dalism" in which a monopolistic Catholic Church was remark-ably weak; whereas in North America, the competition among denominations "produced an unmatched level of individual religious commitment and cultural influence."[21] There is an interesting analogy here between the feudal-hierarchical Church of England and the feudal-hierarchical Catholic Church in Latin America. In both Great Britain and in the U.S., dissenting Protestant denominations were the dynamic congregations of the logic of modernity. Protestant triumphalism proclaimed at the 1910 World Mission Conference in Edinburgh "identified Christianity with modern progress and democracy, and the bur-geoning success of the American ideal and system with its Protestant ethics . . . not only accepted [modernity] . . . but to some extent claimed paternity."[22]

The Catholic Counter-Reformation's preference for an enter-prise association continued to influence the Papacy down to the early twentieth century and this influence sheds light on the sta-tus of Catholicism and Catholics in the United States. As late as 1885, Pope Leo XIII in his encyclical *Immortale Dei* insisted upon Catholicism being the official state religion; in his 1895 encycli-cal directed to the U.S., *Longinqua oceani*, he criticized the American idea of the separation of Church and State and insist-ed that the Church should "enjoy the favor of the laws and the patronage of public authority." This was not a view shared by American Catholics. Nevertheless, Catholic immigrants, along

---

20   Ibid., p. 194.
21   Ibid., p. 197.
22   Paul Johnson, op.cit., p. 462.

with immigrants from Eastern Europe, continued to be viewed with suspicion precisely because there was a real question of whether they did, could, or would share the logic of modernity embraced by American Anglo-Protestants. It was not until after the Second World War that the Papacy fully came to terms with the logic of modernity. This had a profound effect on the role of American Catholics.

American Catholics were able to be acculturated to the larger vision of modernity. This is best reflected in the work of the Jesuit John Courtney Murray, who in the late 1930s and early 1940s was among the first to make the case that Catholicism, in our words, needed to reconcile itself to political civil association. Murray argued for a newer and fuller truth about human dignity, wherein it is the responsibility of all citizens to assume moral control [autonomy] over their own religious beliefs rather than acquiescing in a paternalistic state. In many ways this echoes Locke's *Letter Concerning Toleration*. During the Second Vatican Council Murray drafted the council's endorsement of religious freedom, *Dignitatis Humanae Personae (1965)*. In the intervening period, prominent American Catholic clergy such as Bishop Sheen and Cardinal Spellman became spokespersons for the view that America was a chosen nation with a mission. Contemporary Catholics such as the late Father Neuhaus, Michael Novak, and Father Sirico remain among the most articulate spokespersons for this vision of America.

Summary

We have identified the logic of modernity as involving the relationship among the TP, FME, LG, RL, and CPA. We have indicated how each of these features is a product of the Judeo-Christian heritage. We have shown how America is the historical inheritor and clearest exemplar of that logic, and we have indicated how America is exceptional in maintaining the heritage that supports the logic of modernity as well as making that logic the spiritual quest of modernity.

CHAPTER FOUR

SPIRITUAL CAPITAL AND ECONOMIC FREEDOM

"It is becoming an increasingly obvious fact of economic history that the development of economic systems which concentrate on the common good depends on a determinate ethical system, which in turn can be born and sustained only by strong religious convictions. Conversely, it has also become obvious that the decline of such discipline can actually cause the laws of the market to collapse. An economic policy that is ordered not only to the good of the group – indeed, not only to the common good of a determinate state – but to the common good of the family of man demands a maximum of ethical discipline and thus a maximum of religious strength." – Pope Benedict XVI, *Caritas in Veritate* (2009)

Introduction

There are three explanations of the origins of prosperity. First, prosperity is viewed as the product of magic. Second, prosperity is the product of conquest. Third, prosperity is the rooted in the human creative capacity. The first two views assume that wealth is pre-existing; the third view posits that prosperity can be created by human effort. Spiritual capital reflects the third way. "The kind of knowledge and effort involved, however, cannot be wholly captured by the neoclassical economics assumption of a completely rational, utility maximizing, fully informed *homo economicus*. In the past, attention has focused on financial capital and physical capital as static, limited assets to be accumulated and managed. The source of economic prosperity was taken for granted, largely, as an existing condition to be exploited. In this context, economics was modeled more on the basis of resource management in large systems, with growth and development coming largely from management of costs. Economic growth is not reducible to a mechanical model that can be planned at the macro level. It requires freedom, it requires inspired effort, and it requires commitment to a larger spiritual vision."[1]

Economic development is also, as Peter Berger reminded us in *Pyramids of Sacrifice*, a "religious category." Economic development is clearly a vision of redemptive transformation. "This sense of spiritual capital is founded on an understanding that all resources are entrusted to people. That both individual persons and groups are called to preserve and develop a wealth of resources for which they are accountable here and later and which endowments must be managed. Thus, spiritual capital is about this entrustment of responsibility and a care for the creation it exhibits. Within the Judeo-Christian inheritance, creative obedience or norms in economic activities are one primary way for adherents to acknowledge and demonstrate faith."[2]

America's spiritual capital is reflected economically in three ways. First, there has been phenomenal economic growth associated with the technological project that cannot be explained in traditional ways. Second, Americans are more productive and work harder than their counterparts in other developed national economies. Third, Americans are the most philanthropic people in the history of the world.

How is Judeo-Christian spiritual capital related to economics?[3]

---

1   Malloch and Massey, op.cit.
2   Ibid.
3   See Rodney Stark, op.cit.

Part of the answer depends on how one understands economics. Economics as a discipline is often very helpful, and individual economists often present important insights. However, understood as a pure social science, economics has not generally been useful, and that is for two reasons. First, there are no timeless truths in the social sciences, only occasional useful highly qualified generalizations. Second, economic institutions and practices interact with other non-economic ones. We can neither understand economic phenomena independently of history and other social institutions nor can we reduce our understanding of other social institutions to economics.

Markets and trade, including international trade, have existed from time immemorial. We have maintained that the important historical development was the TP. It is the presence of the TP that accounts for the extraordinary importance of market economies in the modern world. David Hume (historian among many things) and his friend Adam Smith (who held a Scottish Enlightenment view of historical stages) were the first to appreciate the connection between the TP and FME. The connection between economic phenomena and other social phenomena is reflected in Smith's two important works, *The Wealth of Nations* and *The Theory of Moral Sentiments*.

Marx and Marxist economic historians also appreciated the importance of the connection between the TP and the ME, and they did emphasize the connection between economic phenomena and other social institutions. However, their analysis was flawed[4] by (a) a dubious larger philosophical/historical thesis which claimed to be able to predict the future, and (b) a political agenda, both of which led to a host of predictions, all of which turned out to be false, and policies which turned out to be disastrous for humanity. The worst part of their intellectual legacy was introducing the term "capitalism." Capitalism is a theoretical term for Marxists, not a descriptive one. To use the term is to unwittingly accept a lot of objectionable theoretical baggage.

4   See F.A. Hayek (ed.), *Capitalism and the Historians* (Chicago, 1954).

Among the objectionable theoretical baggage is the claim that all social phenomena, including religious beliefs are products of underlying material forces. Using the term "capitalism" is misleading and distorting; the term is an attempt to capture what we have called the logic of modernity, and we think it fails to do so economically, historically, and culturally.

Turning now to the religious side of the equation, Max Weber looms as the major theorist of the relationship. Weber overcame the positivism of both economics as pure science and Marxism by stressing the connection between what we have called spiritual capital and economic growth. In his book *The Protestant Ethic and the Spirit of Capitalism*, Weber[5] maintained that certain denominations of Protestants combined commercial activity with asceticism, not wasteful and conspicuous consumption. They reinvested profits to create greater wealth, and this in turn led to Western domination of the globe. The creation of wealth was now a *calling*, the commercial way of doing God's work in the modern world.

Weber's thesis was insightful but needed serious qualification. Disciplined work and economic productivity as God's calling was an idea that originally developed in medieval Catholic monastic communities. This still underscores the spiritual capital of the Judeo-Christian heritage but puts its origin at an earlier date. John Gilchrist has shown that most of the features we associate with "capitalism" first appeared in medieval Christian monasteries.[6] Other historians have pointed out that all of the features we identify with modern commercial societies were already present in Renaissance (Catholic) Italy.[7]

5   See Randall Collins, *Weberian Sociological Theory* (Cambridge, 1986). We like Collins's observation that Weber disapproved of timeless generalizations and that "Weber's position might well be characterized as historicist . . . seeing history as a concatenation of unique events. . . . Once a crucial conjuncture occurs, its results transform everything else . . . " p. 35.
6   John Gilchrist, *The Church and Economic Activity in the Middle Ages* (N.Y. St. Martin's, 1969).
7   Henri Pirenne, *A History of Europe from the End of of the Roman World in the West to the Beginning of the Western States* (1936); Fernand Braudel, 1977, *Afterthoughts on Material Civilization and Capitalism* (Baltimore: Johns Hopkins)

What we have emphasized is that it is only in the light of the TP and the philosophical reorientation behind it that ascetic reinvestment and serious economic growth go hand in hand. There cannot be this kind of growth in a purely agrarian economy. The TP is a Renaissance and Reformation phenomenon. We have identified the logic of modernity as involving the following: TP → FME → LG → RL → CPA → TP. Each of these features has its origin in the Judeo-Christian world view. This is the extent to which Weber is correct. Some have noted the connection between asceticism and economic productivity in the Chinese Confucian tradition. However, Confucianism has no counterpart to the Judeo-Christian God who creates an orderly and purposeful universe and is therefore the inspiration of the TP!

For all the above reasons, it will be useful to review the historical relationship between the Judeo-Christian tradition and the market economy.[8]

Scripture & Economics

One cannot derive from the Old Testament specific contemporary economic policies. Not only was the economy itself largely limited to agriculture, but economic reflection was necessarily limited to the family and the household. Economic reflection was not applied to society as a whole or to larger political units like a nation, an empire, or the globe.

What we do find are important general moral admonitions. To begin with, there are the Ten Commandments (specific to commerce are the commands to not lie, cheat, steal, or covet). It is hard to imagine any civilized society or institution that does not embrace these norms. In addition, we are urged to work hard, take care of the poor (those who cannot take care of themselves), promote just institutions, and be good stewards of God's creation. Finally, economic gain is not the ultimate purpose of

8   See Max Stackhouse (ed.), et. al., *On Moral Business* (Grand Rapids: Eerdmans, 1995), pp. 37–114.

life (wealth consisted then of land, perishable agricultural products, and jewelry). All of these norms continue to have import but their meaning in specific sets of circumstances evolves over time. We shall, however, identify these moral principles as: (a) basic norms, (b) personal responsibility, (c) social responsibility, (d) poverty problem, (e) environment, and (f) ultimate purpose.

The same can be said of the New Testament. However, there has been a long-standing tendency among some Christian writers to try and derive anti-market policy implications from the New Testament. Careful scholars have made clear just how much this is a distortion of the Gospels. For example, Martin Hengel[9] has pointed out that Jesus saw the root cause of evil in the heart of individuals, not in economic exploitation or political domination. Matthew's parable of talents is not about equality but contractual responsibility. Luke, especially in the *Acts of the Apostles* where he states famously "from each according to his ability and to each according to his need," has served as an inspiration for Marxists, Progressives, and the Christian left to justify some kind of egalitarianism. But scholars now agree that what Luke was discussing and advocating was communitarianism of the Christian community within the Roman Empire and not universal and timeless public policy. "[T]he notion that people simply went out and sold all they had in order to share it with the rest is built on an incorrect interpretation of the Greek grammar."[10] This, of course, would be impossible for the whole society to do anyway because there would be no one to whom to sell. "Christian" Socialism is a figment of the nineteenth- and twentieth-century imagination and has no biblical basis.

Medieval Christian Economic Thought

What is more relevant and interesting in this regard than scripture are the reflections of prominent medieval thinkers on

9   Ibid., p. 81.
10   Ibid., p. 95 (Justo Gonzalez).

economic issues, reflections responding to evolving political and economic conditions. Among such insights is Augustine's claim that the price reflects the buyer as well as the seller; Thomas Aquinas's acknowledgement that profit is legitimate, and Albertus Magnus's assertion (shared by Aquinas) that "goods are worth according to the estimation of the market at time of sale." In 1323 Pope John XXII declared as heretical the Franciscan positions that everything was owned in common and that poverty was essential to Christianity. The Medieval emphasis on the dignity of labor had a profound effect directly on Locke who would go to argue that value was created by human beings who mix their labor with an object.

Of special interest is the debate over usury. In the Old Testament, specifically in Deuteronomy, Jews were admonished not to charge interest when dealing with other Jews, but it was permissible in commercial dealings outside of the Jewish community. Turning to the New Testament, Luke (6:34–35), again, Jesus urged us to "love your enemies, do good, and lend, expecting nothing in return." In response to evolving economic conditions, Christians recognized that it was legitimate to compensate a lender for lost opportunities and permissible to charge interest for purchases made on credit. A conceptual distinction was made, as we do today, between interest – which was legitimate because it contributed to the long-term economic well-being of all, and usury– which was not legitimate because it promoted exploitation and not everyone's economic well-being.[11]

Modernity

We call attention to the importance during the Renaissance and Reformation of the School of Salamanca,[12] among whose

---

11 See Bertrand W. Dempsey, *Interest and Usury* (Washington, D.C.: American Council on Public Affairs, 1943).
12 Schumpeter claims that the School of Salamanca founded economics as a science. This school has also been identified by Murray Rothbard as precursors of the Austrian School of Economics (Mises, Hayek, and Rothbard himself).

members the most significant were the Spanish Jesuit theologians Francisco de Vitoria and Francisco Suárez. They sought to restate the insights of Aquinas in the modern context and in response to Protestant critics. In economics, they defended the free market and recognized that in such a market the just price was determined not by the cost but by supply and demand. They further argued that private property encouraged economic growth. Luis de Molina, another member of the school, noted that private owners took better care of their property than is taken of common property, thereby anticipating the doctrine of the tragedy of the commons.

Already implicit in late medieval and early modern thinking is the notion of economic growth. No doubt the discovery of the new world and sea routes to Asia, aided by the use of the newly developed compass,[13] played a part. But the central issue is that the classical and medieval world viewed the economy as a fixed pie or a potentially shrinking pie. In such a world, poverty is natural and the norm. Hence there is no problem of poverty because that is an unalterable fact of life. In fact, during the medieval Christian period the poor were *sacralized* – viewed as special manifestations of God and objects of concern to the Church. In such a world, anyone seeking a bigger piece of the pie must necessarily take a piece from someone else, hence the necessary expansion of the Roman Empire just to feed its population. Those who seek to improve their economic lives are viewed as greedy – taking something at someone else's expense. "Starting around the time Europe discovered the New World, Europe's economies began a sustained, burgeoning expansion of wealth, unique in history, that continues to this day. During this same period, human accomplishment in the arts and sciences also flourished to a degree unique in history. A connection seems inescapable."[14]

13 The compass was developed simultaneously in Europe and in China, but like gunpowder the Chinese never contemplated its practical use – perhaps because the notion of the technological project was foreign to them and foreign to them because they did not have the Judeo-Christian concept of God.
14 Charles Murray, *Human Accomplishment* (New York: Harper Collins, 2003)p. 332.

Locke[15] took economics out of the private household, where it was placed in the thought of the ancients, and placed economics in the public or political realm. This is the origin of political economy. There is something new about the issues generated by political economy that are different from the quarrels of the ancients. That world argued about virtue and vice, courage and cowardice, excellence and ignorance, innocence and sin, whereas the modern world has as its argument something new, what we have called the liberty narrative and the equality narrative.

In the classical and medieval world the economy was largely agricultural, and even trade was largely confined to agricultural products; populations as well as economies were static. Reflection on such issues revolved around a perspective within which the world was seen as finite, cyclical and teleological, and therefore non-evolutionary and self-contained; there was a finite and no-growth universe. Theoretical economics focused on questions of the just price and the charging of interest.

With modernity the world came to be viewed much differently. Galileo and Newton replaced the Aristotelian notions that rest was natural (wherein motion was problematic) and that motion was circular with the views that motion was natural (hence rest was problematic) and that motion was linear (and therefore evolution and progress were possible). Copernicus changed our perspective from that of a closed world to an infinite universe. Both Descartes and Bacon promoted the idea that wisdom consisted not in conforming to nature but in manipulating it, hence the Technological Project. The voyages of Columbus, da Gama, and Magellan contributed to the notions of growth and expansion. Suddenly, nations were engaged in economic growth, expansion and competition. It is at this point that economies are viewed as operating nationally. Reflection was focused on the Wealth of Nations![16]

---

15   The next few paragraphs are taken from the introduction by Nicholas Capaldi and Gordon Lloyd (eds.), *The Two Narratives of Political Economy* (2010, Scrivener).

16   Precisely because some early modern political economists poured the new

Once the pie is seen as expanding, everything changes, or almost everything. To pursue economic growth is not only to help oneself but to help others precisely because the pursuit of growth expands the entire pie – everyone gets a larger piece. The economy is no longer zero-sum (as in the popular game of Monopoly!). Whereas begging had been institutionalized in the Middle Ages, in the modern period, as reflected in the writings of Luther and Calvin, it came to be viewed as an abuse of public trust and a form of exploiting the industrious members of society. Whereas hoarding was a vice in a world of zero growth, consumerism is the religious vice of an economy of plenty. Consumerism is here understood as the acquisition of resources not because they are aesthetically pleasing or useful for the expression of human values or further growth, but as fashionable symbols of success – symbols in the eyes of others for those who lack autonomy!

The technological project within a free market economy is the greatest engine of economic growth in the history of the world. This growth requires and demands changes in all other institutions – Government, Law, Family, and even Religion. Even what constitutes a virtue gets redefined. Two contemporary scholars have been especially helpful here in explaining the evolution of the virtues. Jane Jacobs[17] contrasts the virtues of a feudal agrarian society with the virtues of a modern commercial society:[18]

Feudal Moral Syndrome	Commercial Moral Syndrome
Shun trading	Shun force
Exert prowess	Come to voluntary agreements

wine into old bottles by adopting *mercantilism* (the view that while wealth was far greater than hitherto imagined it still was finite so that one nation's gain was another's loss), and that is why Adam Smith had to argue against mercantilism.

17 Adapted with changes from Jane Jacobs, *Systems of Survival: A Dialogue on the Moral Foundations of Commerce and Politics* (1994).

18 A good and fun way of observing the contrast is to watch the first scene of the film *The Godfather* in which the undertaker goes to the Don to seek a service. Notice the different conceptions of what a *contract* is, what *friendship* means to the Don. The Mafia replicated in America the feudal system of Sicily.

Be obedient and disciplined	Honesty
Adhere to tradition	Use initiative and enterprise
Respect hierarchy	Respect contracts
Loyalty	Efficiency
Take vengeance	Be open to inventiveness and novelty
Deceive for the sake of the task	Dissent for the sake of the task
Make rich use of leisure	Promote comfort and convenience
Be ostentatious	Invest for productive purposes
Dispense largesse	Thrift
Be exclusive	Collaborate with strangers
Show fortitude	Be industrious
Be fatalistic	Be optimistic
Treasure honor	Compete

Another author, Deidre McCloskey, has written extensively on the virtues of a modern commercial society.[19] Contrasting three different cultural contexts (the Classical Aristocratic Patrician view, Medieval Christian Peasant Plebian, and Modern Bourgeois Mercantile), we see that the first promotes the virtue of *courage*, the second the virtue of *fortitude* in place of courage, and the third promotes *enterprise* (which is a modern combination of courage and fortitude); *justice* in the classical world is superseded by *fairness* in the medieval world and by *responsibility* in the modern world.

Perhaps the most important factor in the economic development of the West has been the extent to which the Judeo-Christian heritage promotes autonomy. "Progress in science in the West has been fostered by enthusiastic, nonstop, competitive argument in which the goal is to come out on top. East Asia did not have the cultural wherewithal to support enthusiastic, nonstop, competitive arguments. Even in today's Japan . . . technological feats far outweigh its slender body of original discoveries. . . . [p]rogress that can be made consensually and hierarchically

---

19　See first her article "Bourgeois Virtue," in *The American Scholar*, Spring. 1994, pp. 177–91; more importantly see her book *The Bourgeois Virtues: Ethics in the Age of Commerce* (Chicago: 2007).

versus progress that requires individuals who insist that they alone are right."[20]

Equality

There is no more contentious political-economic concept than "equality." We shall have more to say about it in the next chapter when we contrast it with "liberty," but for the moment we want to review its odyssey in the Christian tradition.

The Judeo-Christian heritage is the origin of the concept of equality, with Christianity specifically proclaiming the equal moral worth of all persons in the eyes of God. Drawing both on Stoic doctrine and Genesis we find that all human beings "male and female" were created in the "image of God." This doctrine of equality as expressed by Paul (*Galatians* 3.26–29) is that, "There is neither Jew nor Greek, there is neither bond nor free, there is neither male nor female: for ye are all one in Christ Jesus."

The Protestant work ethic promoted the notions of the inner-directed individual, the emphasis on work or achievement, equality before the law, and differentiation based on achievement. Protestants were willing to concede an arrangement in which the political realm was not subordinate to the religious realm as long as the political realm was obliged to respect the traditional spiritual realm of Christianity. Here we see the beginning of the tensions between liberty and equality.

For Protestants the spiritual realm was now understood to mean the opportunity to do God's work by economically transforming the world and all of its attendant circumstances. Equality before the law came to mean that there should be no

---

20   Murray, p. 399. Murray refers to Richard Nisbett from *The Geography of Thought* (2003): ". . . properly raised Chinese or Japanese children have made their crucial life decisions with the wishes and welfare of their parents, then of their extended family, and then of their community in the forefront of their minds. Nothing in either Chinese or Japanese culture encouraged the maturing child to focus on his own ideas and ambitions and seek out ways to fulfill them no matter what." Murray, p. 397.

legal barriers to economic activity that did not apply equally to everyone. Placing legal barriers to equal participation in the economic realm was to thwart God's plan! One consequence of this conception of equality was meritocracy. In its Protestant form, meritocracy was not just a reflection of personal merit but of divine preordination. After all, it was God who inspired us and accounted for the differences in achievement. At the same time, higher status was accompanied by a sense of greater responsibility, not the privileges of self-indulgence.

Equality before the law was an expression of Christian liberty. This Calvinist notion of political and legal equality influenced the Dutch, British, and American Revolutions. The Calvinist influence in the English Civil War is reflected in a group known as the "Levellers." The Levellers comprised the rising middle classes, small property owners, tradesmen, artisans and apprentices. In one pamphlet, John Lilburne asserted the notion that no one has authority without consent. In the famous debate held at Putney in 1647, speaking on behalf of the Levellers, Colonel Rainborough asserted that "the poorest he that is in England hath a life to live as the greatest he"; no one is obliged to obey a government "he hath not had a voice to put himself under." At the same time, the Levellers wanted to deny the franchise to all those whom they considered lacking in moral independence, such as almstakers and house-servants.

The more radical group was the "Diggers." Their spokesperson, Gerrard Winstanley, rejected private property as a reflection of original sin. His claim was that "one man hath as much rights to the earth as another." He went on to attribute the existence of poverty to exploitation by the rich, and advocated a form of agrarian communism.

The difference between the Levellers and the Diggers heralds the ongoing dialectic in the development of modern notions of equality. What we see here is the difference between equality of opportunity and equality of result. Equality of opportunity is the position that a practice is unjust if it fosters inequality of treatment based upon irrelevant differences. Equality of result is the advocacy of a total equality that entails a collective conception of the good in which the individual good is subsumed. The Levellers challenged the political power structure but not the economic and social system. This was a consistent expression of Calvinism and the commitment to doing God's work in an increasingly market-oriented society. The Levellers adhered to the Platonic-Augustinian view that we live in two cities, so that given original sin this world would always be an imperfect reflection of the City of God. Poverty was a consequence of a lack of moral independence that itself reflected original sin. On the other hand, the Diggers reflected the medieval Anabaptist call for complete equality within a feudal agrarian economy still committed to the notion of a collective good. The Diggers believed that some sort of social utopia was possible here on earth.

Writing a century later, David Hume made the following critique of radical equality and fairness. First, there was no agreement on what these concepts meant. That is, they seemed to be a rhetorical flourish rather than a serious position. Second, distributing resources to those who could use them best required a kind of knowledge that humans did not possess (anticipating Hayek). Third, if resources were redistributed equally, this would soon lead to a new inequality once people began employing (or wasting) those resources. Fourth, in order to maintain the original equal redistribution we would need a new form of absolute tyranny.

We shall have more to say about "equality" in the next chapter.

Poverty

A market is a dynamic process that evolves in unpredictable ways over time. Part of a properly functioning market is competition, a competition in which there will be winners and losers. It is not the market that fails, but of necessity individual businesses within it will fail. In all of this, the consumer remains sovereign, for it is in the service of consumers that businesses toil. The people who own or work for the failed businesses do not fail; on the contrary, they move on to other occupations provided by the previous winners who expand the economy, or they start new business ventures and enter the competition again. Today's winners are not necessarily tomorrow's winners; today's losers are not necessarily tomorrow's losers. The only person who always wins is the sovereign consumer of an expanding economy. Not everyone seems to be emotionally or psychologically capable of living in such a world.

The lack of autonomy explains the existence of dysfunctional people in free societies. The standard diagnosis (usually this means the politically correct explanation) for the existence of dysfunctional people is the lack of resources or the lack of positive rights. The default remedy is some form of redistribution. On the contrary,[21] the existence of these dysfunctional people and a whole host of social problems is a reflection of the presence of people who have not yet developed a sense of personal autonomy.[22] This is true both domestically and internationally. The greatest obstacle to globalization is the resistance to cultural change that seeks to substitute the notion of personal autonomy for more collectivist conceptions of the self. There are those who argue that this amounts to Western cultural hegemony. But in reality, autonomy is a fundamental truth about human nature, and its prevalence in the West is a result of the Judeo-Christian inheritance. Those non-Westerners who have experienced and

---

21 This explanation is borrowed from Michael Oakeshott's discussion of autonomy in "Masses in Representative Democracy," where he identifies the dysfunctional as anti-individuals.

22 Gertrude Himmelfarb's two books, *The Idea of Poverty* (1983), and *Poverty and Compassion: The Moral Imagination of the Late Victorians* (1992), show the transition from the early nineteenth-century view that poverty was a moral problem involving individual responsibility (Charles Booth) to the twentieth-century view via the Fabians that the poverty problem is really a social problem about the equality of the working class.

embraced personal autonomy recognize that it is an irreversible transformation of the self. Autonomy is not one choice among many, for the very notion of choosing an identity only makes sense if we have the capacity for autonomy. Finally, cultures are not rigid structures but historical artifacts that change over time, most especially when confronted with alternative cultures.

The global hope of achieving drastic poverty reduction is hinged on what has been termed the Millennium Development Goals (MDGs). These goals were set and agreed to by the international community in 2001, to establish objectives for the period to 2015 during which time significant improvements would be achieved in eight broad areas – poverty, education, gender equality, child mortality, maternal health, HIV/AIDS and other diseases, environmental sustainability, and global partnerships for development. There seems to be a convergence of opinion among scholars that with what has been achieved so far, and what is required to meet set targets, the hope of attaining the MDGs is actually quite remote.

Why is that so? We think that the concept of poverty alleviation and wealth creation cannot be separated. Indeed they are intertwined such that one is an extension of the other. Poverty alleviation is simply about "lifting" the poor out of poverty. This connotes survival– having to meet the basic survival needs of individuals.

This can be summarized to mean giving a man fish in order for him to survive. This is because policy initiators viewed poverty simply as material deprivation. Thus attacking it, the attention of government had focused on helping the materially deprived (the poor) to alleviate his/her condition. Wealth creation, on the other hand, is all encompassing. It entails the following:

a. Teaching the man how to fish (by inculcating requisite income-generating skills).

b. Showing the man the way to the river.

c. Making available the necessary tools required for fishing.

d. Ensuring that there is demand for his excess catch.

e. Providing other ancillary services that will be required by the man to ensure that he can maximize his "catching" potential. It is worth pointing out that (b-e) focus on *empowerment*. Poverty is only overcome when people are empowered and allowed to help themselves without undo influence from others and particularly from the government and its agencies.

American Exceptionalism

American exceptionalism is the view that the United States occupies a special role among the nations of the world in terms of its national ethos, political and religious institutions, and its being built by immigrants.

The roots of the position date back to 1630 with John Winthrop's "City Upon a Hill," although some scholars also attribute it to a passage of Alexis de Tocqueville, who argued that the United States held a special place among nations, because it was the first working representative democracy.

Belief in American exceptionalism has typically been more characteristic of conservatives than liberals. The radical Marxist Howard Zinn said that it is based on a myth, and that "there is a growing refusal to accept" the idea of exceptionalism both nationally and internationally. By contrast, many conservatives have argued that to deny American exceptionalism is in essence to deny the heart and soul of this nation.

In essence the exceptionality of America, politically, economically, militarily, and culturally, is based on:

1. Protestant American Christians' belief that American progress would lead to the Christian Millennium.

2. American writers also linked their history to the development of liberty in Anglo-Saxon England, even back to the

traditions of the Teutonic tribes that conquered the Western Roman Empire.

3. Other American writers looked to the "millennial new-ness" of America, seeing the mass of "virgin land" as promising an escape from the decay that befell earlier republics.

Because America lacks a feudal tradition of landed estates with an inherited nobility, it is arguably unique among nations. The Puritan Calvinists who first came to Massachusetts had a strong belief in predestination and a theology of Divine Providence that has effects to this day. Since God made a covenant with his "chosen people," Americans are seen as a different type. This "City on a Hill" mentality is still evidenced in American folklore, song and customs. With its particular attention to immigration, America has generation after generation been a beacon to the world. The Statue of Liberty is an embodiment of that ethos. America was also created on a vast frontier where rugged and untamed conditions gave birth to the American national identity and the narrative of exceptionalism.

The economics of the American founding[23] was very much a Lockean affair: the protection of property rights in what was "the largest contiguous area of free trade in the world." But there were two competing views of America's economy: a Southern agrarian view, championed by Jefferson, and a Northern industrial and commercial view, championed by Hamilton. It is this same difference in visions that was at the economic root of the Civil War, a war that ultimately saw the industrial and commercial view victorious.

Hamilton, as Secretary of the Treasury, prevailed. He established the credit of the United States by consolidating state and national debt and paying the interest upon it, and transforming it into capital by issuing certificates on it; he established a nation-

---

23 Forrest McDonald, "The Founding Fathers and the Economic Order," in Stephen M. Klugewicz and Lenore T. Ealy (eds.), *History, On Proper Principles: Essays in Honor of Forrest McDonald* (Wilmington, DE: ISI Books, 2010), pp. 263–69.

al banking system; and he thereby encouraged what he called "the spirit of enterprise." Hamilton "used the freedoms of the Constitution and its protections to create a capitalistic, free-market economy and ensured that the United States would become the richest, most powerful, and freest country the world has ever known."[24]

The role of the government in such an economy has been well described by James Madison in *Federalist Ten*:

. . . the most common and durable source of factions, has been the various and unequal distribution of property. Those who hold and those who are without property, have ever formed distinct interests in society. Those who are creditors, and those who are debtors, fall under a like discrimination. A landed interest, a manufacturing interest, a mercantile interest, a monied interest, with many lesser interests, grow up of necessity in civilized nations, and divide them into different classes, actuated by different sentiments and views. The regulation of these various and interfering interests, forms the principal task of modern legislation, and involves the spirit of party and faction in the necessary and ordinary operations of government. . . . [t]he *causes* of faction cannot be removed; and that relief is only to be sought in the means of controlling its *effects*. . . . [a] pure democracy . . . can admit of no cure for the mischief of faction. . . . A republic . . . promises the cure for which we are seeking. . . . [t]he same advantage, which a republic has over a democracy in controlling the effects of faction, is enjoyed by a large over a small republic.[25]

In order to be a fit participant in a modern market society it is necessary to be a certain kind of person in a certain kind of culture.[26] We have previously identified that culture as the commercial moral syndrome. What kind of person internalizes its values

24 Ibid, p. 269.
25 George W. Carey and James McClellan (eds.), *The Federalist* (Indianapolis: Liberty Fund, 2001), pp. 44–48.
26 Writing in 1947 in the aftermath of the Second World War, Ludwig von Mises in his classic work *Human Action* (Indianapolis: Liberty Fund, 2007) asserted

and makes it work? It is no accident that Weber identifies none other than Benjamin Franklin as the epitome of the Protestant work ethic! Nor is it an accident that America is the most philanthropic country in the world.[27]

both that "The social philosophy of the Occident is essentially a philosophy of freedom" (p. 284) and that "the immense majority of our contemporaries are mentally and intellectually not adjusted to life in market society, although they themselves and their fathers have unwittingly created this society by their actions. But this maladjustment consists in nothing else than in the failure to recognize erroneous doctrines as such" (p. 319).

27 See *The Puritan Gift* by Kenneth and William Hopper.

CHAPTER FIVE

SPIRITUAL CAPITAL
AND POLITICAL FREEDOM

"[T]here is a great tradition of warnings in presidential farewells . . . are we doing a good enough job teaching our children what America is and what she represents in the long history of the world? Those of us who are over thirty-five or so years of age grew up in a different America. We were taught, very directly, what it means to be an American. And we absorbed, almost in the air, a love of country and an appreciation of its institutions. If you didn't get these things from your family, you got them from the neighborhood, from the father down the street who fought in Korea or the family who lost someone at Anzio. Or you could get a sense of patriotism from the popular culture. The movies celebrated democratic values and implicitly reinforced the idea that America was special. TV was like that, too, through the mid-sixties. . . . But now we're about to enter the nineties and some things have changed. Younger parents aren't sure that an unambivalent appreciation of America is the right thing to teach modern children. And as for those who create the popular culture, well-grounded patriotism is no longer in style. . . . We've got to do a better job of getting across that America is freedom. . . . And freedom is special and rare. It's fragile; it needs protection." – Ronald Reagan, *Farewell Address*

Introduction

We live in a society that subscribes to the political norms of classical liberalism: market economy (private property), limited government (liberty), and the Rule of Law. The norms of classical liberalism are *procedural* norms, that is, they do not specify particular collective outcomes but the manner in which we pursue our private individual agendas. In addition to participation in the procedural norms, each (most) of us participates in *substantive* moral communities (religion, family, etc.) that provide content-full norms or substantive moral visions; it is the fulfillment of these norms that gives deep meaning to our personal lives. The substantive norms promote respect for the procedural norms. There are some differences in our substantive commitments (e.g., religion), but as long as each and every religion promotes respect for the procedural norms and as long as there is religious toleration, a liberal society can flourish.

Mediating structures are where people live their lives. Between the individual and the all-powerful state lie a series of human institutions that Burke called the "little platoons." Others like Berger and Neuhaus in their important short book, *To Empower People*, see these institutions as necessary for life and abundant human flourishing. They need to be protected, encouraged and enlarged and not discredited and obliterated, as much of modern policy has done. These institutions make up the basic units of life – the family, the school, the churches, voluntary organizations and what in more recent terminology have come to be known as "civil society" or what used to be called civic life. Much attention has been given to how these institutions might thrive again and why without them we as a people will wither and die while the State comes to usurp all power and crowd out these mediating structures. American spiritual capital is largely about these institutions, their survival and their empowerment.

The major thesis of this book is that without the Judeo-Christian heritage and its spiritual capital, there will be no support for the procedural norms. The minor thesis is that the Judeo-Christian heritage has itself flourished best within a politically free society, as opposed to a theocracy. This is the ultimate significance of the Augustinian doctrine of the Two Cities, and it is the very thing that John Courtney Murray explained in such a way that Catholics could become part of the mainstream of American culture.

How do Judeo-Christian religions do this? They encourage recognition of personal freedom and responsibility that we know as *inner-directedness*; they insist upon the separation of religion from politics in order to protect the sanctity of spiritual (personal) life (Augustine); and they promote *trust* (if we share some substantive norms we are likely to trust that others will abide by the same procedural norms).

Reference is made here to the assimilation of Catholics into the mainstream of American culture (whose origins are mainly Anglo-Dissenting-Protestant) because it can serve as a model for what will happen in the assimilation of Islam. Criticisms of Islam and pointing out the potential tensions between Islam and the mainstream of American culture are not intended as Islam-bashing. It is worth noting that there are those who (a) hope to see American transformed into an Islamic culture, or (b) make it politically incorrect to identify these tensions not because they espouse Islamic (or any religious) hopes but because they wish to use Islam as a stick with which to attack the Judeo-Christian inheritance, or (c) are mindless espousers of cultural diversity because they are just plain ignorant about the Judeo-Christian inheritance and the tensions generated by other cultural inheritances.

The Two Narratives of America[1]

So far we have told a particular version of the story of America with special reference to its spiritual capital. But not everybody tells the same story. In fact, there have always been two main narratives that people tell about Modernity: the liberty narrative and the equality narrative. Both of these narratives

---

1   Much of this is taken from Nicholas Capaldi and Gordon Lloyd (eds.), *The Two Narratives of Political Economy* (Salem, MA: Scrivener/Wiley, 2010).

as we have pointed out earlier derive from the Judeo-Christian heritage; both are initially articulated within the Enlightenment; and both of these narratives evolved during the nineteenth and twentieth centuries. Both of these narratives compete to serve as America's spiritual capital.

The reader may question why we are about to devote so much time to Locke and Rousseau in what purports to be an account of the two narratives of America. The answer is that (a) Locke (later Hume and Smith) is the direct influence on the founding; and (b) the proponents of what we call the equality narrative have always taken their intellectual cue from the continent of Europe, not Great Britain, and they have no interest in the Founders except to dismiss them as "dead white males who owned slaves."[2] It is reflected today in those who want the U.S. to become like the European Union, a functional integrated secular unit.

The following discussion of the two narratives will also help to explain another phenomenon: the debate over which history of America will be taught in public schools. One narrative will presume that Columbus's discovery and the European settlement of the new world is on the whole a good thing and that the world is a lot better off because the founders preserved and extended both the Judeo-Christian heritage and British political institutions. The other narrative will argue that the European settlement was an invasion that destroyed a wonderful indigenous culture(s), that the only good things about America were the products of the pre-Columbia inhabitants,[3] that the founding was an economic swindle (e.g., "Progressive" historians: Charles Beard, Carl Becker, Frederick Jackson Turner), and that the entire Cold War was the result of U.S. intransigence and megalomania as well as paranoia.

---

2   Thomas G. West, *Vindicating the Founders: Race, Sex, Class, and Justice in the Origins of America* (2000).

3   See Jon Butler, Dean of the Graduate School of Arts & Sciences and Howard R. Lamar Professor of American History, Yale University, *In Becoming America: The Revolution before 1776* (2007). Butler argues against a predominantly British identity of colonial America.

Readers who have grasped the point about the nature of narratives will not be surprised.

Locke's Liberty Narrative

The first version takes its bearing from the natural rights and social contract teaching of Locke, and its common sense Scottish companion: it focuses on individual liberty and equality of opportunity in the economic, political, and religious dimensions. It is more at home with competition and consent rather than what it saw as the monopoly and coercion forces operating in economic, political, and religious life. It is no accident that in its seventeenth- and eighteenth-century versions, there was in this competitive-consensus model, an interrelated opposition to the monopoly inclinations of "inherited" property accumulation under feudalism, the "divine" concentration of political power in a monarch, and the dominance of the Papacy, or any other conforming tendencies in Christianity. The Protestant origins of this narrative can be seen in the promotion of the inner-directed individual, the emphasis on work, equality before the law, differentiation based on achievement, and the right of individual conscience. The insistence upon equality before the law is rooted in the notion of Christian liberty. Adam Smith and James Madison both rely on the link between liberty and competition on the one hand, and choice and consent on the other in making the case for the three aspects of freedom.

There is an equality component to the liberty narrative, namely, equality of opportunity and equality before the law, that is thoroughly compatible with liberty as expressed in the following truth: all men are created, or born, equal, and thus have the individual right to life, liberty, property, and the pursuit of happiness. Equality before the law means that there should be no legal barriers to economic activity that did not apply equally to everyone. The liberty narrative assumes the equal autonomy of human beings as a normative point of departure, and the challenge is to secure individual liberty as an empirical reality. This task will, for a variety of legitimate reasons, produce unequal outcomes.

The early defenders of the liberty narrative emphasized the superior efficiency of a free market over and against government regulation and ownership. Nevertheless, the narrative is grounded in a moral claim that compulsion is unfair and wrong. The moral core of the liberty narrative was stated as truths in the United States *Declaration of Independence* by way of Locke: "all men are created equal, that they are endowed by their Creator with certain unalienable Rights, that among these are Life, Liberty and the pursuit of Happiness." Life is understood as the necessary condition for liberty and liberty is the means by which individuals pursue happiness. The religious origin and grounding of this narrative should be apparent.

Rousseau's Equality Narrative

The second version takes its bearing from the natural rights and social contract teaching of Rousseau, and its utopian companion in the French Revolution, and focuses on community, solidarity and equality of outcome in the economic, political, and religious dimensions. It emphasizes the vices of competition such as selfishness, greed, fraud, luxury, and anarchy. What pulls this second narrative in the direction of equality of outcome is the human sense of compassion. And there is an analogue in politics and religion: an emphasis on the rule of the general will rather than the rule of law and the substitution of a civil religion, or secular humanism, for the rule of individual conscience. Whereas the liberty narrative favors a civil association, the equality narrative favors an enterprise association.

This second version as it developed from Rousseau, through Marx, to the Progressives and FDR, to the New Left, to the Great Society and beyond has a very hard time accepting the unequal distribution of income and wealth that comes and goes with the presence of competition. The suspicion that there is something fraudulent about the distribution of property by means of competitive markets carries over into the political and religious realms. There is a critique of the competitive system of separation of governmental powers between three branches, the deliberative dimensions of representative democracy, the federal division of powers that encourages deliberation and discourages action, and even the presence of religion as "an opiate of the people." There is in this second narrative a different conception of the role of government, especially what government should do and which level of government should do it. What sustains the attractiveness of the equality narrative is a moral claim that inequality is unfair and wrong. In one form or another St. Simon by way of Rousseau stated the moral core of the equality narrative: "from each according to his ability, to each according to his need." Or in the language of the Declaration of Rights of the French Revolution: "Liberty, Equality, Fraternity." Liberty is the necessary condition for equality and equality is in turn the means to secure fraternity.

The Liberty Narrative Expanded

The claim of the adherents of liberty is that a free market economy is the most effective means of carrying out the Technological Project, the conquest of nature in the service of human needs. The dynamic of the Technological Project requires constant innovation, and the free market economy maximizes such innovation through competition as well as specialization. That is the claim of "classical economics." The classic theoretical argument for the centrality of a free market was made by Adam Smith in the *Wealth of Nations* (1776). Smith emphasized private property, competition, and the division of labor – all of which contribute to technological innovation. But Smith was also the author of *The Theory of Moral Sentiments*, suggesting that some sense of individual responsibility and common good is connected to the increase in the production of the necessities and conveniences of life.

Smith replaced Locke's natural law framework for liberty

with a natural history approach. Like other Scottish Enlightenment thinkers he explained the emergence of liberty as part of the stages of economic growth. Smith, following his friend Hume, replaced the centrality of reason (understood as the mirror of nature) with imagination – a reflection of the inner-directed individual. It was through imagination that we could adopt a social perspective both to restrain our partiality and to sympathize with the interests of others. Rather than proclaiming pure enlightened self-interest and rather than dismissing Rousseauean protests of inequality, Smith attempted to deal with the distribution issue through sympathy and the "hidden hand." The same God (understood Deistically) who created an ordered universe hospitable to human interest created individuals who could be sensitive to the interests of others and whose pursuit of their own interest coincidentally fostered the interest of others. God's order was discovered not in physical nature but in the social world and the individual sensorium.

Protestants especially saw an important connection between politics and economics. The connection between politics and economics derived from the fact that government controlled large parts of the economy by granting privileges such as monopolies, sinecures, land grants, etc. Political equality implied economic equality in the sense that all possessed the liberty to pursue God's work in this world. This is the sense in which the government is subordinate to the requirements of commerce. Commerce provides the infrastructure that enables competition between the opinions, passions, and interests in society so that the outcome is as close to the preservation of liberty and the securing of justice as is possible to expect. This economic or commercial foundation, where we have the competition of economic, political, and religious interests in an "extended orbit," is the necessary condition for securing liberty. Nevertheless, we need government. Free government, in contrast to good government or a general will government, is characterized by the *rule of law*. According to the American Founders, a political and legal system that *constrains the excesses of popular government,* while retaining the essence of popular government, is said to exhibit the rule of law. But we need to remember that the rule of law is not the same as the law of rules. In a Republic, the rule of law is typically embodied in a Constitution, which provides protection for rights within the very structure of government, and a Bill of Rights that specifies those rights against the overreach of government. The rule of law involves the right of the people to elect their representatives, and it also includes the separation of powers and checks and balances on a majority that is tempted to tyrannize an economic, political, or religious minority.

The rule of law has evolved jurisprudentially into a system of rules designed to allow individuals to pursue their self-defined interests without interfering with that same pursuit on the part of others. As Hayek was to express it, *the rule of law provides the rules of the game without determining the outcome of the game.* As elaborated by Michael Oakeshott, the rule of law exists only in a civil association, that is, one in which there is no collective good, only the good of its individual members. The law prescribes conditions to be observed by individuals who pursue their own purposes, alone or with others. The laws are neutral with regard to whether the purposes are achieved. If, on the contrary, the law is construed as an instrument for achieving particular economic or political objectives, the rule of law is violated or disappears.

It is a government of laws and not of men. We can't simply trust men in power to do the right thing and expect liberty to prevail, unless precautions are placed on their conduct. As Madison put it: "if all men were angels, no government would be necessary." But we add with swiftness: if all men were beasts, free government would be impossible. Free government in all three spheres of liberty – political, economic, and religious – supposes the ability of individuals to govern themselves, at least most of the time on the most important matters pertaining to their life, liberty, and pursuit of happiness. Through the give and take of competition, "the deliberative sense of the community" should prevail. There is no temptation in the liberty narrative to

turn men into angels and thus eliminate the need for government. That would mean that no government would be necessary, and it would mean the end to the liberty narrative. The liberty narrative is not a utopian anarchist narrative.

In Madison's view, there is no *collective* good to be imposed
by an outside authority of experts or central planners, but there
is a *common* good that emerges from the deliberative process.
The common good consists of what happens when the conditions (e.g., rule of law, toleration, protection of individual rights,
reliance on markets, separation of powers, etc.) are right for the
expression of liberty and within which individuals pursue their
self-interest. This restates Adam Smith's invisible hand simile
and anticipates Hayek's theory of spontaneous order: if you
leave people alone to pursue their own self interest – within the
confines of the rule of law – then the common good is more likely to emerge than if imposed from the outside by an all-knowing
expert.

Attempts to promote direct democracy as a basic form of
organization encourage people to discover their nastiness and to
act on it. The Framers of the United States Constitution followed
the eighteenth-century fashion of decrying direct democracy and
placed their faith in the idea of a "Republic." In the nineteenth
century, Tocqueville in *Democracy in America* (1835) warned about
the "tyranny of the majority," a theme taken up by J. S. Mill in his
essay *On Liberty* (1859). And the twentieth century has also found
thinkers like Hoover, Hayek, and Friedman who have defended
the liberty narrative over and against the equality narrative
because of their concern that an overbearing majority encouraged by egalitarian supporting intellectuals and bureaucrats will
undermine the rule of law and thus the empire of liberty.

The Equality Narrative Expanded

Rousseau represented an important and often overlooked
and misunderstood counter-current; the kind of equality that
counted, for him, was moral equality. This kind of equality could

be threatened by economic inequality (*Discourse on the Origins of Inequality* in 1754), and in the *Social Contract* of 1762 he urged that no one be "so rich as to be able to buy another, and none so poor as to have to sell himself" (II, 11). His *Political Economy* introduced the concept of the general will, a concept vital for the collectivist political project presented in the *Social Contract*.

In the *Discourse on the Arts and Sciences,* Rousseau critiqued the Technological Project. Instead of satisfying genuine human needs, the arts and sciences are expressions of pride (promoting invidious self-comparison), and they have led to luxury and the introduction of human inequality. In the *Discourse on Inequality,* Rousseau suggested that the division of labor and the institution of private property are antagonistic to the perfection of human beings because, to anticipate the theory of justice propounded by John Rawls, not everyone enters the social contract "naked" as it were, or with a "veil of ignorance." Rousseau critiqued the liberty narrative in the two discourses; in his *Discourse on Political Economy*, he introduced the "general will" as THE principle of political economy; finally, in his *Social Contract* he provided a robust political account of the general will, which will is implemented and sustained by an appeal to civil religion.

The Lockean social contract, as seen from the *Rousseau-through-Rawls* lens in the twentieth century, is viewed as a fraud, if it ever actually took place at all! It is a fraud, first, because the few who were rich and powerful *forced* the less fortunate many into institutionalizing inequality. Rousseau's social contract is meant to remedy this political and social inequality by requiring everybody to give up everything when, again anticipating John Rawls, they enter civil society not knowing what is in store for them ahead of time. It is a fraud, secondly, because no such event has actually taken place in empirical reality. This notion that certain privileged folks are putting one huge something over on us victimized many is central to the equality narrative.

The Rousseau narrative transforms the Lockean conception of rights from the rights of the individual to the rights of the community. Under the Rousseau model, each individual gives up each and all rights upon entering society. Each person enters stripped of rights and, naked, abandons all attachment to a previous and stunted private self and acquires a new and grander public self. The general will replaces individual choice; obedience becomes total rather than conditional. If you revert to a yearning for individual identity and personal autonomy, then it is the appropriate role of government "to force you to be free." In the Rousseau narrative, individual rights are only *prima facie*, may be overridden, and may be possessed by any entity, not just individual human beings. Such rights can be welfare rights, i.e., they may be such that others have a positive obligation to provide such goods, benefits or means.

Rousseau's critique of modern society, especially the idea that private property was theft and that limited government is contrary to true and pure democracy and the general will, was adapted and broadened in the nineteenth century (e.g., Marx) mainly by writers we now identify generically as "socialist." These writers, unlike Rousseau, were more willing to embrace technology, but they criticized the poverty, inequality, alienation and degradation which, they alleged, were consequences of the Industrial Revolution. They focused on the unfairness – the inequality – of the distribution of the goods and services generated by the new technological world. They advocated the abolition of private property, which they asserted had unfairly concentrated power and wealth among a few, and did not provide equal opportunities for everyone. But they sought not merely more equal opportunity; rather, they defended more equality of outcome. And they articulated a scientific basis for this moral critique: just as capitalism came into being, it shall go away either as a result of some immanent law of evolution, with the revolutionary conduct of the united working class.[4] All will be well in the end; no government will be necessary because all men will have become angels.

---

4   Cloward & Piven, The Weight of the Poor: A Strategy to End Poverty, *The Nation* (May 2, 1966).

Despite the claim to be scientific, the equality narrative has been criticized for its romanticism. In *The Roots of Romanticism*, Sir Isaiah Berlin identifies the romantic roots of the equality narrative: "[Romanticism] introduces for the first time . . . a crucial note in the history of human thought, namely that ideals, ends, objectives are not to be discovered by intuition, by scientific means, by reading sacred texts, by listening to experts or to authoritative persons; that ideals are not to be discovered at all, they are to be invented."[5]The fundamental basis of romanticism is will, "the fact that there is no structure to things, that you can mould things as you will – they come into being only as a result of your molding activity – and therefore opposition to any view which tried to represent reality as having some kind of form which could be studied, written down, learnt, communicated to others, and in other respects treated in a scientific manner."[6] Again, as Berlin writes, "there is even such a thing as romantic economics . . . where the purpose of economics, the purpose of money and trade, is the spiritual self-perfection of man, and does not obey the so-called unbreakable laws of economics. . . . Romantic economics is the precise opposite of [laissez-faire economics]. All economic institutions must be bent toward some kind of ideal of living together in a spiritually progressive manner."[7]

The Rousseau narrative has expanded in many different directions. It was used in the eighteenth century by small landowners and agricultural workers against large feudal landowners, and in the nineteenth century by worker movements against employers who owned factories. It has been used by inhabitants of former colonies who were educated in the West, against former colonial powers.[8] It has been used by some African-Americans against whites, and some feminists against perceived domination by white males.

5 Isaiah Berlin, Roots of Romanticism (1965), (London: Chatto & Windus, 1999), p. 87.
6 Ibid., p. 127.
7 Ibid., p. 126.
8 See Ian Buruma and Avishai Margalit, *Occidentalism* (Penguin 2005).

Reflections on the Two Narratives

The proponents of the equality narrative yearn for a return to the collective identity of the ancient polis, or what Oakeshott called the view that society is an enterprise association. The equality narrative depends on the case for the acceptance of strong government and for the very same reason: a general will generates communal fraternity and this trumps the individual pursuit of happiness. Whether in the Marxist and strong socialist form of government ownership of the means of production, or the softer socialism and Progressive agenda of greater government regulation of the private sphere of life (especially the relationship between capital and labor), or planning for a more rational and fairer society in FDR and the Great Society programs, the equality narrative relies on government being the solution rather the problem, and the non-governmental sphere is the problem rather than the solution. The equality narrative contains a liberty component, namely, liberation from insecurity, fear, disease, hunger, and misery that is compatible with the emphasis of the equality narrative on equality of outcome as a normative goal and empirical reality. And this will inevitably lead to restraints on individual liberty. Think of the recent debate on healthcare.

There is no sentimental notion of equality in Marx or contemporary intellectuals, but there is a form of absolute egalitarianism. The workers would clearly not be equal to the planners, but it is assumed that this appearance of inequality would not be onerous or invidious in light of the collective good because the workers and the planners have a common bond. Somehow or other differences of function would not translate into differences of status in light of the collective good.

And this leads us to the phenomenon of the American Progressives who are clearly not Marxists. True, they also thought that a regime dedicated to the preservation of property was an undemocratic regime because private property is only owned by the few. And, yes, they wanted to separate politics from administration and rely on the latter rather than the former. But they were not revolutionary nor did they endorse the idea of "inevitability" concerning the case for equality. There was to be no end to the history of Progressivism. The Progressives thought that through cooperation, rather than competition, in the fields of both politics and economics, we could settle the disputes between labor and capital without having a revolution or ignoring social justice. They sought to rid politics of the influence of special interests, to rid economics of the influence of economic royalists, and to turn voluntary charity into "the administration of things." They sought to replace the world perceived as consisting of unbridled self-interested competition with the world of detached public interest administrators, allegedly produced by universities with schools of public policy. We can replace the old narrative of liberty (which was only for the few) with the new narrative of equality (which is for the public good).

The New Deal and the Great Society programs extended the Progressive approach to "the social question." This social question is not simply that the market economy is inefficient and not delivering food and shelter to the public. Rather, at the core of these problems is a concern with the fundamental fairness of life. The forgotten man, the ordinary folk, has been the victim of the greed of the unrestrained few. It is the role of government to initiate recovery and invite the people to engage in a rendezvous with destiny. The liberty narrative has failed the promise of democracy, and it is the duty of government to overcome this crisis. Look at FDR's speeches as well as LBJ's Michigan Address on the Great Society, and you will see that both are presented as crusades to eliminate domestic evils and both appeal to the sense of social justice.

Let us return now to the liberty narrative. The increasing call for an absolute equality, now understood as the call for the recognition of a collective good – equality and fraternity – that subsumed the individual good, raised the same alarm in the nineteenth century that it had in the eighteenth century. Critics such as Tocqueville and Mill left a set of writings that warned of a conflict between equality and liberty.

Tocqueville urged that serious attention be given to the inclination of modern man to choose equality with slavery over liberty with inequality. He also warned that modern man also had a great inclination to support the centralization of government which, given the history of the French Revolutions of 1789, 1830, and 1848, is the way to tyranny. Later, Hayek will identify this as "the road to serfdom." In part, this reflects the desire of modern man to "belong" in a world that had lost the hierarchical connections of the ancient world. Tocqueville encouraged the development and protection of intermediate institutions, like local political, economic, and religious associations, that actually support the goal of individual liberty. He called this self-interest rightly understood as: by helping others, you help yourself. Self interest wrongly understood is: by helping myself, I help others.

The advocates of a collective good in which individual good is subsumed do not see the necessity for preserving liberty, because the purpose of liberty in their eyes is to lay the foundation for equality-as-fraternity. Rather they insist upon controlling any institution and practice that contributes to individual fulfillment within the collective good. Liberty, for them, is the necessary condition for equality, which is the avenue to fraternity. Defenders of liberty, on the other hand, justify removing or relaxing external constraints because they presume that there is some kind of basic internal psychological need for something like personal autonomy. The defenders of liberty are reasserting in secular fashion the Christian doctrine of the dignity of the individual soul. This is what is behind J. S. Mill's defense of individuality. The case for individual liberty is that it is the condition for the individual pursuit of happiness.

The argument in favor of individual liberty and against fraternal equality is sometimes presented as an efficiency argument. The efficiency argument goes something like this (diagram below assumes no inflation and constant purchasing power).

Society A represents where we are now.

Society B_1 represents where we would be if current proposals for increasing the welfare state and redistributing income were put into effect.

Society B_2 represents where we would be if absolute equality were imposed and maintained.

Society C represents where we would be if we did away completely with income transfer schemes. Note that in Society C, the bottom 20% are much better off than they were in Society A in an absolute sense (remember the value or purchasing power of the dollar remains the same) but the gap between them and the middle 70% has grown wider. It might be pointed out that the numbers here are exaggerated. Even so, the point remains the same.

A	B_1	C
10% earn >$1 million	100% earn $40,000	10% earn >$10 mil.
70% earn $50,000	B_2	70% earn $1 million
20% earn <$20,000	100% earn $200,000	20% earn $100,000

Defenders of absolute equality relative to a collective good make the claim that even if there were a net loss of economic benefits, the non-economic social benefits (e.g., the lack of envy) would far outweigh that loss. It has also been suggested that if the wealthy voluntarily chose to redistribute their wealth to the less wealthy or to the poor there would be no loss of wealth and a lot less misery as well as more happiness. However, this suggestion (as an example of romantic economics) fails to take into account that such a voluntary redistribution would affect future productivity. For example, a poor person is likely to spend the boon on immediate gratification whereas the wealthy person might reinvest that surplus in creating new industries and jobs. In fact three-quarters of the wealth of the wealthiest individuals is invested in such ventures. The defenders of absolute equality respond by claiming that the poor engage in immediate gratification only because they have been victimized. And thus the argument proceeds.

Some advocates of the liberty narrative have also critiqued the pure efficiency argument. In the early nineteenth century, Constant, in his famous essay *The Liberty of the Ancients compared to that of the Moderns,* voiced a concern later to be echoed in Tocqueville. Constant deplored the fact that so many intellectuals were mistakenly hostile to religion, and he opposed Rousseau's idea of a civic religion. Constant advocated religious toleration, not only to check centralized power but also because he believed that the truths individuals would find within religion, if not coerced, were essential both to true human fulfillment and to the preservation of liberal culture as a whole. A liberal polity had to be both secular and tolerant; a liberal culture needed to be deeply religious. Similar arguments will be made by Daniel Bell, Irving Kristol, Peter BErger, and in Catholic Social Thought.[9]

Defenders of individual liberty sometimes present their argument as an argument in favor of freedom or autonomy (understood here as self-rule or self-governance). Even if there were no net economic loss, there would be an end to freedoms such as speech, thought, religion, and the right to choose the government under which we live. We would witness the triumph of mediocrity or a narrow public opinion imposing the same capricious and arbitrary standards on everything and everyone. These freedoms are important because they are instrumental to personal autonomy and the pursuit of happiness. For Tocqueville and Mill, freedom trumps efficiency and that is why they are sometimes, incorrectly, identified with the egalitarian narrative. They believed that the defense of liberty required more than the case for efficiency.

For Tocqueville and Mill – just as it had been for Locke,

---

9   Daniel Bell, *The Cultural Contradictions of Capitalism* (Basic Books, 1976); Irving Kristol, *Two Cheers for Capitalism* (Mentor, 1978); Peter Berger, *The Capitalist Revolution* (Basic Books, 1988).

Smith, and the Founders, and just as it will be for Hoover, Hayek, and Friedman, freedom of choice trumps fraternal equality. Wealth is important neither as an end in itself nor as a means to consumerism, but because it serves as the means for personal accomplishment. This is the argument of the liberty narrative. Wealth maximization and efficiency considerations are important because we need to know if such policies are maximizing opportunities for more and more people to become autonomous. Public policies that redistribute wealth are permissible only to the extent that they ultimately promote autonomy. Redistribution is not *a priori* objectionable if it promotes autonomy as well as efficiency.

With regard to current public policy debate, the major assumptions of the Liberty narrative are:

(1) individual liberty is the most important value

(2) anything that promotes liberty also promotes efficiency

(3) growth is potentially infinite

(4) absolute poverty will be overcome by growth

(5) "relative" income or income gaps are non-issues because

(6) autonomous individuals are focused on self-defined achievement and self-respect – do not define themselves in terms of others

(7) "dysfunctional" members of a free society blame others either because they harbor private grievances or because they lack the courage and self-discipline to become autonomous. Intellectuals who speak on behalf of the alleged "victims" either suffer from the same character defects or because it is a mask for a private agenda in which they see themselves as the future elite (new clerisy of the enterprise association).

The major assumptions of the Equality narrative in the contemporary scene are:

(1) self-esteem and the need to feel equally a part of a larger social whole are the fundamental human needs, and this is not possible without considering who we are relative to others within a social context

(2) there are limits to growth being ignored by those who are

despoiling the environment, and the economic focus should be on sustainability

(3) sustainability requires "fair," "rational" and politically responsible rationing and regulation

(4) the pursuit of autonomy leads to anomie or is a mask for private self-aggrandizement

Many people, particularly on this side of the Atlantic, have never heard of Wilhelm Röpke. That is a shame, since he is one of the most important economists of the twentieth century, a true Renaissance man, a polymath, and a father of the German economic miracle. He displayed unique moral courage, was often politically incorrect, and was perhaps the sharpest critic of Keynesianism. Ludwig Erhard claimed he "illegally obtained Röpke's books . . . which I absorbed as the desert drinks life-giving water." Röpke, a full professor at the age of 24, was also the first German professor to lose his job in 1933 when the Nazis came to power. As an exile who would not cave in to Hitler and the SS, he never returned to his native land. He is less well known to the English-speaking world than Hayek, Mises, or Friedman.

Röpke's contribution to intellectual life breaks new ground, is highly readable and adds considerably to the economic literature. It should become mandatory reading for every student of political economy. It is essential for the articulation of liberal economic reasoning.

As the intellectual author of Germany's post-World War II economic resurrection, Röpke is an underappreciated thinker who informed policy-making. He can rightly be called a Smithian, as he was against the unlimited power of the state. Put positively, he was much more. Röpke was an "economic humanist" of the first order. He historically showed how the Great Depression came to limit economics as a science and how collectivism is incompatible with authentic human freedom.

Röpke focused on four subjects. They are: the challenge of business cycles, the unending growth of the welfare state, employment and inflation, and international economic relations. Röpke's political economy was attuned to 'interdependence,' where empirical analysis is not separated from normative judgment. With a focus on "human flourishing," Röpke was enlightened beyond today's narrowly trained economists and econometricians because of his scope and vast intellectual and multidisciplinary horizons. By returning modern economics to the Aristotelian realm of ethics from which it originally emerged, Röpke achieved a new synthesis. For him the market economy allowed people to exercise their natural liberty – rooted in the Christian realism of St. Augustine.

As part of the Austrian School, as opposed to the Historical School, Röpke can be best placed in the context of other major modern economic thinkers such as Eucken, Rustow, Böhm and Miller-Armack. Breaking with the dirigisme past, together they sought to articulate an economy rightly framed on order. For them economics was a normative social science. They discerned values beyond utility. This is a style of political economy that needs to find a revival as it is sorely lacking in today's boring mathematicized journals and small-gauge discussions about trends in data.

For Röpke, economics has unfortunately occupied a "restricted vision." This view parallels the better-known thoughts of Hayek, who likewise warned about the scientism of economics and was an equally harsh critic of Lord Keynes and his overly ardent followers. Both witnessed what they called "the failure of intellectuals" and their near total surrender to the evils of socialism portrayed as a "road to serfdom" inhabited, if not dictated by government bureaucrats.

With liberty constantly under attack, Röpke's "Christian Humanism" is a perfect antidote or remedy to the crisis that abounds and surrounds us on every front. It appears that even in our most recent economic collapse and massive government interventions cum bailouts we are plagued with an incessant belief in what Röpke termed "the folly of human perfectibility."

It is absolutely correct to make the connections to the Scottish Enlightenment thinking in Röpke's opus. Röpke sought to avert welfare statism but held a conservative attachment to tradition, especially to the mediating structures of civilized life. The space between the individual and the all-powerful state is where life is actually lived.

This conflict with what could be called classical liberalism and the priority of freedom in the economic realm continues today. Ordoliberalism owes a great debt to the Scottish Enlightenment. And the tension between social conservatism on one side, and economic liberalism, even in American and continental politics on the other, continues into our present era. Until it is resolved – perhaps by reemploying the likes of Röpke or his seminal ideas, we will be one-handed and fail to see the full dimensions of ordered liberty. Such division also undercuts political power, dividing it into warring camps. A cohesive model of the social market economy offers a viable alternative.[10]

Role of Religion

The equality narrative to be sure draws on the Judeo-Christian inheritance just as the liberty narrative does. Nevertheless, the part of the tradition on which egalitarians draws, has always been viewed as heretical. As we have pointed out in previous chapters, the Church has always found it necessary to reign in utopian and egalitarian movements. That is why there is a marked tendency for proponents of the egalitarian narrative to drift toward or to advocate a secular viewpoint. Rousseau's promulgation of a civil religion is a prime example. Those clergy who lose or never had their faith in the transcendent

10 Guided by the thoughts of Alexis de Tocqueville, Samuel Gregg's *The Commercial Society* identifies and explores the key foundational elements that must exist within a society for commercial order to take root and flourish. Gregg studies the challenges that have consistently impeded and occasionally undermined commercial order. He reminds us that commercial order is about much more than the market economy. He identifies the central moral, legal, and economic foundations of market orders and illustrates why they are indispensable to any society that aspires to the title of free and civilized.

easily drift in this direction as well – for them the state replaces a church.

At the same time, we have noted that some proponents of a purely efficiency argument for liberty have often felt uncomfortable with the appeal to religion. The appeal to pure efficiency and done in the name of science has two liabilities. First, efficiency always concerns means and can never by itself legitimate an end – hence the tendency to obscure the difference between *liberty* as the absence of external constraint and *freedom* as internal autonomy. These are the people who especially love the technical Hayekian argument against planning but who feel uncomfortable about their "faith" in spontaneous order. Second, the drift toward scientism coalesces with the equality narrative's attempt to scientifically plan economies.

In order to make clear the assumptions and implications of the two narratives, we shall contrast the fundamental religious values of American culture that underpin the liberty narrative with the norms of what we shall call the post-American narrative.

A. Fundamental Religious Values of American Culture
1. View of Human Nature
   a. Free will – individual human beings are ultimately responsible for what they do.
   b. Sin – human beings are born with destructive as well as wholesome impulses and becoming a decent person is a life-long struggle and achievement. Intermediate institutions such as the family and religion help us to gain control of ourselves.
   c. Rights (Negative)
      i. In its Lockean formulation, rights reflected a Judeo-Christian moral-religious conception of the relation between the individual and God.
      ii. In its original Lockean formulation, these rights (e.g., life, liberty, property, etc.) are absolute, do not conflict, and are possessed only by individual humanbeings. Rights are morally absolute or fundamental because they are derived from human

nature and God, and as such cannot be overridden; the role of these rights is to protect the human capacity to choose. Finally, such rights impose only duties of non-interference.

   iii. The purpose of these rights is to limit government; the responsibility of government is to refrain from violating your rights and stop others from violating your rights.

2. View of Civil Society (including the economy)
   a. Free Market economy – the "Business of America is Business"
   b. Religion
      i. America began as an Anglo-Protestant culture (Samuel Huntington, *Who are WE?*).
      ii. The Judeo-Christian heritage is the core of America's spiritual capital; it has made possible our economic and political achievements and freedoms; these achievements cannot be sustained without that heritage; the heritage has important positive implications for commerce both nationally and globally.
      iii. Judeo-Christian spiritual capital has been the source of the spiritual quest of modernity; that quest has evolved into globalization; and America, because of its spiritual capital, has been able to provide leadership for that quest.
      iv. Islam is problematic to the extent that it does not have a concept of sin and a conception of the separation of Church and State.
   c. Family
      i. Within the family individuals are bonded together immediately through love and affection. Family relationships, unlike those in civil society, are altruistic, not calculating or instrumental. The will of individuals is subordinated to the good of -the institution – hence it is an enterprise association. It is the attempt to create a real and enduring community of wills.

ii. Marriage is not really a contract so much as an agreement to transcend contract.

    iii. Parents do not strictly have personal rights over their children, rather they have obligations to educate them out of childishness and into becoming autonomous. This requires a certain measure of authority which is indeed irresistible, but it is also limited, and forfeitable if abused.

    iv. Children cannot be claimed or treated as property, but they do not have the right to resist instruction.

    v. The recognition of this enterprise association, the family, gives marriage its true ethical significance (hence, merely living together is not enough). The perfect manifestation of this community is children.

  d. Tocqueville on intermediate institutions

    i. Civilian and political associations are a counterbalance to both individualism and the centralization of the state. Intermediate institutions are where individuals learn to work both for a collective good and the common good and where individuals are protected from the power of the state.

3. View of Government

  a. Authority, ultimately, comes from the consent of the governed.

  b. American exceptionalism

    i. America has a special world historical role to play because it is the greatest force in the modern world; it has transformed and continues to transform the moral landscape by improving the material conditions of life and by institutionalizing individual freedom.

  c. Civil association

  d. Republic not democracy

  e. The right to bear arms is not a rationalization for moronic militias but reinforces that rights are natural and not given by the state; moreover, individuals are morally obliged to resist a tyrannical state.

4. View of Law & Legal Profession
  a. Common law explication recognizes that we are defined by our traditional practices and those practices are fertile sources of adaptation.
  b. The legal profession should be a conservatizing force in the culture.

B. Norms of Post-America Advocates

1. View of Human Nature
  a. Naturally good; corrupted by the environment
  b. Environmental determinism
  c. Rights (Positive)
     i. Rights are means by which the State enables the natural goodness of human beings
     ii. As such, rights are only *prima facie*, may be overridden (e.g., life is now defined by the courts), and may be possessed by any entity (e.g., groups, animals, etc.), not just individual human beings. Such rights can be welfare rights, i.e., they may be such that others have a positive obligation to provide such goods, benefits or means.
     iii. This conception of rights vastly expands the power of government.

2. View of Civil Society
  a. Regulated economy
  b. Anti-religious – deeply suspicious of religious institutions (e.g., schools) precisely to the extent that they promote the assumptions and values that diverge from the post-American view; religious toleration becomes a mask for an anti-religious agenda
  c. Anti-traditional family – same reason as (b) above

3. View of Government
  a. Ultimately, authority comes from the collective goal of the community as vouchsafed by the "appropriate" intellectuals
  b. Post-American
  c. Enterprise association[11]

---

11   Ronald Dworkin, in *Law's Empire* (Harvard University Press, 1986), speaks of law as "fraternity, community" and "conceptually egalitarian," p. 198–201.

> d. Democratic socialism
>
> e. Anti-gun
>
> 4. View of Law & Legal Profession (radical and adversarial)
>
> a. All law is legislation ratified by a majority

The norms of a post-American view are reflected in the structure and curriculum of U.S. universities[12] in general and most current U.S. law schools. What follows are the list of what we call the ten commandments of U.S. law schools.

1. Law School Education: The Constitution was written by dead, white males who owned slaves and therefore is to be ignored. The only parts of the Constitution that deserve to be taken seriously are the amendments (especially one, two, and fourteen) plus the *Miranda* decision.

2. Law School Graduates: There is no such thing as free will, or sin; human beings are born good and corrupted by their environment; hence, the only way to solve problems is through an all-powerful federal government that forces institutions to function properly. The federal government is to regulate and oversee the delivery of all services, and it is to be staffed by law school graduates (Administrative Law).

3. Law School Faculty: Anyone who does not subscribe to the above views is incompetent and obstructionist and therefore ought not to be hired, promoted, or given tenure.

---

12 The hostility of intellectuals to modern commercial societies is well documented. See Joseph Schumpeter, *Capitalism, Socialism, and Democracy* (1975); Bertrand de Jouvenel, "The Treatment of Capitalism by Continental Intellectuals," in *Capitalism and the Historians*, ed. F. A. Hayek (1974); Ludwig von Mises, *The Anti-Capitalist Mentality* (1975); Peter Klein, "Why Economists Still Support Socialism," *Mises Daily Article* (11/15/06); Robert Nozick, "Why Do Intellectuals Oppose Capitalism?" *Cato Policy Report* (1998). See Paul Hollander, *Political Pilgrims: Western Intellectuals in Search of the Good Society* (1997). Philosophy, for many, is the articulation of a moral vision for those hostile to substantive religious communities. What intellectuals most despise about modern commercial societies is that such societies are not enterprise associations requiring a clerisy – namely a special role for themsevles as leaders.

4. Law School Students: The pursuit of efficiency and excellence are excuses for racial, ethnic, and sexual discrimination. Equality of opportunity and equality before the law are to be replaced by equality of result (Affirmative Action). Diversity is to be encouraged in all things but no one may challenge the 10 Commandments. "Diversity" means students should look different but should think the same. "Diversity" does not apply to faculty viewpoints.

5. There is no value left in traditional American economic institutions such as private property. On the contrary, progressive taxation, eminent domain, but most especially the EPA, SEC, EEOC, OSHA, HEW, etc., will eliminate all of it. *Environmentalism* is the new socialism. Again these agencies will all be staffed by law school graduates. Do not waste your time studying contracts or going to work for a private law firm.

6. The major social institutions of American society (family and Church) are passé. Marriage must be redefined and religious institutions that promote traditional Judeo-Christian beliefs and practices are to be systematically dismantled. Middle-class values are to be replaced by a new morality of alternative life-styles.

7. Traditional political and legal institutions such as federalism, local control, and the rule of law are to be replaced by law as legislation, a new social contract as defined by John Rawls and Ronald Dworkin.

8. Domestically, crime cannot be handled by allowing citizens to bear arms and by police and prisons, but only by greater economic and social equality.

9. Internationally, the use of military force is always wrong (but most especially by Republican administrations).

10. We live in a Post-American world, i.e., the nation state, but especially the U.S., is to be replaced by a new world order. The Constitution and case-law (*stare decisis*) are to be replaced by international and trans-national law.

Where Are WE?

After years of booming business and unbelievable wealth creation, the economy has slowed and stalled, stunned by a mortgage crisis and a near financial collapse (2008) that has only reinforced the notion of big businesses as insatiable masters of the universe with little regard for the public. The critics of capitalism have emerged from every corner to harangue those who create wealth with charges of greed, thievery, and malice.

In *Spiritual Enterprise*, we explored the opportunity of doing virtuous business – a concept that has been disappearing from our public consciousness. Such virtuous business is rooted in spiritual capital. We have argued that the creation of wealth by virtuous means is the most important thing we can do for ourselves and for the world at large. More than simply explaining why enterprise makes the world a better place, the spiritual capital of the Founders' DNA continues to inform and instruct the firms. It can be documented how virtuous business models have made many of the brightest companies in America more successful than ever.

Spiritual enterprise as a business rationale for and evidence of spiritual capital rehabilitates the idea of big business as a force for good in society and offers a sensible guide for realizing this ideal. As anti-globalization and anti-corporate tides are rising, this argument is both a much-needed defense of free enterprise and a vital call for better business.

CHAPTER SIX

THE CHALLENGE OF SECULARIZATION

"The present age is a critical one and interesting to live in. The civilization characteristic of Christendom has not disappeared, yet another civilization has begun to take its place. We still understand the value of religious faith. . . . On the other hand the shell of Christendom is broken. The unconquerable mind of the East, the pagan past, and the industrial socialist future confront it with equal authority. On the whole life and mind is saturated with the slow upward filtration of a new spirit – that of an emancipated, atheistic, international democracy." – George Santayana, *Winds of Doctrine*

Secularization

By *secularization* we mean the loss of religious authority and support for economic, political, legal, and social institutions, and its replacement by non-religious or even anti-religious world views. Conventional wisdom, following Weber, used to ascribe this "disenchantment of the world" solely to the rise of modern science beginning with eighteenth-century Enlightenment rationalism and exacerbated by Darwinian biology in the nineteenth century. More recent scholarship has shown the relative superficiality of this view (e.g., Charles Taylor's *A Secular Age*).

To put this in proper historical perspective we note:

1. Jaspers noted the existence of an "Axial Age" as the origin of most major religions in India, China, and the West (between 800 and 200 B.C.).

2. Polytheism never disappeared.

3. Classical Greek philosophy (and its derivatives) has always been one alternative to a religious outlook in the Middle East as well as in the West.

4. The earliest Christian communities did not articulate themselves in Greek philosophical terms. Those communities were characterized by their faith in Jesus Christ and in their hope of his return. They did not have or require a formal philosophical rationale. It took two centuries before the force of circumstance, the need to defend themselves and to engage in proselytizing, required them to adopt the habits of an alien intellectual world. Second, whereas the discovery of the psyche by the classical Greeks led them to seek attunement with an invisible and impersonal order beyond the visible order, Christians went beyond that in opening themselves to the revelation of God's grace. In the beginning, then, it can be said that Christianity distanced itself from Greek philosophy.

5. Medieval Christians starting with Augustine "rationalized" Christianity by appeal to Greek philosophy (Plato). A number of prominent contemporary Christian thinkers have reasserted the primacy of spiritual experience and have maintained that the sterile metaphysics originating in Parmenides is the "original sin of metaphysics."[1]

6. The rediscovery, or rather reintroduction into the West, of Aristotle's philosophy in the eleventh century was quite another matter. Aristotle's metaphysics is in important respects an improper vehicle for Christianity because it immediately and always invites a purely naturalistic reading. Averroes of Cordoba, an Arab commentator on Aristotle, exercised enormous

---

1   See the work of Fernando Rielo, www.rielo.com.

influence on the early introduction and understanding of Aristotle in the West. Averroes maintained that (a) God is so self-contained that individual human actions are not guided by divine providence, (b) the material world is eternal and not created, (c) the material world is further governed by an internal necessity under the influence of celestial bodies, (d) there was no first human being, (e) the individual soul dies with the body, and (f) the human will acts within material necessity. This view will haunt modernity.

7. For the last two hundred years the dominant intellectual force in Western civilization has been the philosophical and scientistic narrative known as the *Enlightenment Project*.[2] The cosmic order was de-divinized and naturalized. It was now to be accessed through science, specifically by social scientists who formed the new clerisy. The secularization of the process of accessing the cosmic order was accompanied in time by what can only be called a reaffirmation of the centrality of politics and the state and the marginalization of the moral domain.

The Enlightenment Project is, curiously, a Christian heresy. The Enlightenment accepted large parts of traditional Judeo-Christian morality. What it attempted to do was to provide a secular-scientific basis for it. The Enlightenment replaced authority, faith, and tradition with reason. It also identified reason with physical science. In so doing it transformed morality. For example, the Enlightenment denied the doctrine of original sin and insisted that human beings were fundamentally good. A purely Newtonian conception of God as the creator of order would have had it no other way. All natural impulses were good, and if evil resulted from them it was because of environmental influences that had perverted the innately good natural impulses.

Social technology was the attempt to engineer those environmental conditions that promoted the innately good impulses. The notion of the Christian moral will practicing self-restraint as

2   See N. Capaldi, *The Enlightenment Project in the Analytic Conversation* (Boston: Kluwer, 1998).

well as personal responsibility disappears from this view. This particular heresy is even embraced by a large number of clerics, especially at universities with a religious affiliation! One specific and crucial function of the social sciences was to provide a "scientific" account of why other individuals both refused to accept the project and why they stubbornly clung to religion, or to metaphysics, or to tradition. In short, part of the ideological role of the social sciences is to delegitimize the opponents of scientism. Religious studies programs in most universities, as opposed to theology, are social scientific studies of religious "phenomena" largely carried out by non-believers!

According to Enlightenment Project scientism, the world consists ultimately only of objects, and a putative subject must be a concatenation of sub-objects. There is no place in this scheme for the Christian conception of the personal self or a soul. There is no place in this scheme for the Christian conception of the freedom of the will. The foregoing conception of freedom leads to a political conception of ethics based on external social sanctions instead of morality (which involves the inner sanction of autonomous agents). There is no place in this scheme for the Christian notion of personal responsibility. Autonomy is reconceptualized as informed consent where "informed" means causally conditioned by realist, external, and trans-cultural structures. There is no place in this scheme for the Christian notion of "grace."

The proponents of this view see themselves as having triumphed. But this is because it is the ascendant view among ruling elites in Brussels and the other capitals of Europe, Western media, the entertainment industries, and politicized universities on both sides of the Atlantic.

8. Nineteenth- and twentieth-century reaction to the Enlightenment among intellectuals took predictable forms. Pope Leo XIII returned to Aquinas; Nietzsche called for a renewal of the classical Greek philosophical tradition. In the twentieth

century Husserl,[3] Strauss, and Heidegger all called for the same classical revival.

9. Throughout the eighteenth, nineteenth, and twentieth centuries there have been major religious revivals known as "Great Awakenings."[4]

10. The foregoing is meant to show that in the West (a) for centuries there has been an ongoing conflict between various religious narratives on one side and various secular (what we shall call naturalistic or scientistic) narratives on the other side; (b) except in the minds of some elitists, we do not live in a secular age – but we do live in an age of conflict!

Charles Taylor's discussion of secularism is an important scholarly contribution to the complex historical sources of secularity and to its intellectual limits. What is more important is what Taylor does not say here but has expressed elsewhere in his long corpus of writings. Taylor is a serious Catholic who makes a case for the ongoing significance of spirituality. However, Taylor, in his heart of hearts, subscribes to what we have called the Rousseau/Marx narrative, which he disguises as a form of Hegelianism. He reflects a kind of Christian socialism. Taylor is openly an ideologue of the left, specifically, one who holds that we should be living in a society that is an *egalitarian* republic.

---

3   In his 1935 lecture, "Philosophy and the Crisis of European Humanity," Edmund Husserl asserted: "There are only two escapes from the crisis of European existence: the downfall of Europe in its estrangement from its own rational sense of life, its fall into hostility toward the spiritual into barbarity, or the rebirth of Europe from the spirit of philosophy through a heroism of reason that overcomes naturalism once and for all."

4   See Joseph Tracy, *The Great Awakening* (1842), refers to 1730. The second awakening refers to the first half of the nineteenth century and saw the rise of Baptists, Methodists, and Mormons; the third great awakening refers to religious revivals in the last half of the 19th century, marked by social activism and missionary work throughout the world; the fourth great awakening (see Robert Fogel, *The Fourth Great Awakening & the Future of Egalitarianism*, [2000]) refers to the last half of the twentieth century – needless to say in the current climate of post-modern historical scholarship the existence of this "awakening" is challenged.

As an ideologue, Taylor rails about how great inequalities are unacceptable. We are never told exactly what makes inequality bad or exactly when it becomes "great." Taylor ran for election five times in his native Canada as a Socialist candidate, so his political ideology is a matter of public record.

Taylor is part of a long line of philosophers who have tried to revive the notion of an ancient community in the modern world. It is therefore no accident that he begins with Aristotle (who was no true friend of commerce) and admires Catholic medieval monastic life, which was an attempt to instantiate the classical ideal. Nor does Taylor explain why he is a radical egalitarian when that certainly was not a classical or Aristotelian ideal. Taylor recognizes that there are practices that do not conform to his ideal, namely market practices. He thinks these practices are wrong and that they reflect mistaken theories. He calls these alleged theories behind the distasteful practices "atomism" and the "contribution principle." Taylor fails however to see that what really animates us in modernity are the technological project, market economies, limited government, the rule of law, and the promotion of personal autonomy. He also fails to recognize the inherently conservative character of this form of social understanding or how it more adequately reflects the Judeo-Christian inheritance, what we have here framed as its spiritual capital. The last thing Taylor wants to conserve is a commercial republic. His values are socialist, not capitalist.

Religion vs. Scientism

As ideal types, philosophy (understood in its naturalistic and scientistic sense) and religion (Abrahamic traditions) present us with two different narratives.

Philosophy's narrative is monistic and *naturalistic* (the world is fully intelligible in its own terms); *rationalistic* (everything is in principle conceptualizable); impersonal (the ultimate principles of intelligibility have no direct reference or concern for human welfare); and *secularly pelagian* (despite the impersonality, humanity can solve its problems on its own).

Religion's narrative is *dualistic* (we can only make sense of the world by appeal to something supernatural); *mysterious* (there is an ultimate mystery at the heart of the universe, a pre-conceptual domain that is not itself conceptualizable); *personal* (the supernatural pre-conceptual ground of our own existence is a person who cares for us); and involves grace (humanity needs divine aid in order to deal with the human predicament). We take this opposition to be perennial. Both sides would offer differing accounts about why the other side never gets the point. Today, atheism has become increasingly militant.

We turn our attention first to the philosophical (scientistic) narrative, a narrative that challenges our basic starting point and forms the basis of a formidable (secular materialist) narrative that stands in an adversarial relation to the narrative we wish to defend. The most influential version of the philosophical narrative today is scientism. Scientism is both the view that (a) the physical sciences, including biology, are the whole truth about everything, and (b) there can be social sciences that explain the human and social world in a manner analogous to the way in which the physical sciences explain the physical world.

What is most remarkable about the philosophical-scientistic narrative is that its adherents hardly recognize that it is a narrative. To begin with there are a host of questions to which physical and social science have no answer. The adherents of this view make the claim that in the future all of these questions will either be answered or delegitimized. That sounds *prima facie* plausible, but such plausibility is purchased at a high price. The price is that adherents must accept that at present they are offering a narrative about what is going to happen in the future and in the face of present ignorance. This belief about the future is not a scientific fact about the future but a fact about an act of faith on the part of those who subscribe to scientism. This is what makes it a narrative! This does not of itself make it a bad narrative, but it does underscore that it is a narrative.

Having once come to terms with the fact that scientism is a philosophical narrative, adherents make the claim that it is more plausible than the religious narrative. We shall spare the reader a long disquisition,[5] but the facts are that (a) there is no intellectual superiority to the scientistic narrative, and (b) no one even knows how to present a plausible defense of the philosophical superiority of the philosophical-scientistic narrative. This point has been made in a variety of ways: all proofs or explanations start with premises that cannot be proven; positivists cannot verify the principle of verification; we cannot even show that science is progressing, that is, that later explanations are better than earlier explanations;[6] the two most important philosophers of the twentieth century, Wittgenstein and Heidegger, coming from different traditions, nevertheless both *show* that the pre-conceptual domain cannot be conceptualized.

How can we make such sweeping claims? What is less remarkable is the extent to which the philosophical-scientistic narrative has nevertheless prevailed in some influential circles. Science in its modern technological form has been so successful in giving us control over nature that the ordinary mortal hardly thinks to question anything that invokes its mantle. We too think that science has to be appreciated and taken seriously, but what we are challenging is scientism, not science. Even the ordinary well-read and intelligent thinker hardly has the time to delve into the complexities of philosophical argument. There is apparently even less need to do so when the academic leaders of this most demanding of intellectual disciplines proclaim the alleged truth of scientism.

We make the following responses to this predicament. First, the philosophical-scientistic narrative cannot intellectually legitimize itself. That is, it not only fails to live up to its own

---

5   See Capaldi, op.cit.
6   Thomas Kuhn, in the *Structure of Scientific Revolutions*, rightly analogizes the embrace of a new theory over an older theory as akin to a religious conversion.

standards but is seemingly possessed of irresolvable tensions. It is defective as well as unsupportable. Second, we can explain why an intellectually defective narrative, defective by its own standards, has been so socially acceptable, and this would not be the first time in history that such is the case. Aside from what we have already said, we shall argue later that the scientistic narrative is a mask for the private political agenda of secular intellectuals who have a great deal to gain personally from its dominance.

Worse yet, the scientistic philosophical narrative has led to the narrative of protest. Briefly, this is how. Historically, modern physical science originated in the West under the influence of the Christian conception of the world in which an all-powerful and benevolent God creates a world that is both orderly and benevolently disposed to its inhabitants. Given these basic assumptions science can proceed both to search for objective order and to expect practical benefits from the search. Without this set of assumptions, science loses its own supportive foundation. Moreover, in its implacable opposition to Christianity, the Enlightenment Project construes the history of science as a movement away from and in opposition to Christianity rather than recognizing the Christian foundations of modern physical science. The Enlightenment Project rejects those assumptions and then is surprised to discover that science lacks foundations.

The narrative of protest is also known as the post-modern narrative.[7] Post-modernism is the view that there are alternative or competing narratives, not an authoritative narrative. Whereas

7   Jean-Francois Lyotard, "Introduction: The Postmodern Condition: A Report on Knowledge," 1979: xxiv–xxv. "Simplifying to the extreme, I define postmodern as incredulity toward metanarratives. This incredulity is undoubtedly a product of progress in the sciences: but that progress in turn presupposes it. To the obsolescence of the metanarrative apparatus of legitimation corresponds, most notably, the crisis of metaphysical philosophy and of the university institution which in the past relied on it. The narrative function is losing its functors, its great hero, its great dangers, its great voyages, its great goal. It is being dispersed in clouds of narrative language elements—narrative, but also denotative, prescriptive, descriptive, and so on [. . .] Where, after the metanarratives, can legitimacy reside?"

scientistic fideists cling to the notion of a scientifically accessed cosmic order, post-modernists consign scientism to the same trash bin as metaphysics, religion, and tradition. Post-modernism denies the existence of a cosmic order that is not another human construction. Post-modernists are more consistent than scientistic fideists because the former see, as the latter frequently do not, that scientism is a humanly constructed narrative. So far, so good! But here is where the narrative of protest goes wrong. Whereas advocates of scientism appeal to a mythical progressive historicism, advocates of post-modernism see in history a gradual "emancipatory" move away from the notion of a cosmic order. Scientism is the last stage in the great emancipation.

But from what are we emancipated? What is the great emancipation an emancipation from or to? If no narrative is authoritative, why embrace an emancipation narrative? Why embrace any narrative? *Why not just be nihilistic?*

Unlike earlier existentialist philosophers, the contemporary French philosophers Michel Foucault and Jacques Derrida do not reject scientism but argue that mathematical science is the only defensible ideal construct for thinking. They seek to interpret the implications of the situation to which the scientific ideal has led. If science is radically relativistic, then everything is radically relativistic. Relativism is a view that had long been asserted on other grounds, but the demise of scientism gave relativism a new lease on life. Their argument is as follows: if no narrative is legitimate then everything is up for renegotiation. *But why should anyone negotiate?*

Doesn't the idea of "negotiation" presuppose a prior (hidden) context or agenda?

What is that hidden agenda? We are back to the equality narrative! This narrative actually originated with Rousseau and was made canonical by Marx. Beyond the common moral critique, there is no agreement on exactly how to transform the present system and what the precise structure of the alternative will look like. What identifies someone as a proponent of this narrative is

(a) the sense of being in an adversarial relation (of varying degrees) to whatever they take the present system to be, (b) the moral critique, (c) the advocacy of restructuring, and (d) the failure to provide an explicit account of how the new structure will function. They are voices of grievance (and hope) without an explicit plan! In a very important sense, the Enlightenment Project leads to this kind of *nihilism*.[8] This approach delegitimizes everything including itself.

Contemporary discussions of the relationship between science and Christianity are often focused on the conflict between Darwinists and Creationists. The effects of Darwinism surround us. It is not even a theory of particularly great scientific erudition. As post-Darwinians and other biological theories about human evolution have unfolded it is clear that there is ample room for contrasting theories, some based in natural science and others in natural law or even natural theology. While we are not proponents of what has been termed Intelligent Design in any of

8   In *Whose Justice? Which Rationality?* (1988), MacIntyre developed his theme of cultural cacophony, but also defended a special kind of Aristotelianism – the Thomistic theistic version, as the most coherent account of the moral life and its justification. He sets forth the thesis that some traditions are superior to others. His criterion is that a tradition is superior to others if it can resolve the problems and anomalies in those other traditions in such a way that supporters of the other traditions can come to understand why they cannot resolve those problems using only their own intellectual resources. MacIntyre illustrates this by showing how Aquinas' synthesis of Aristotelianism and Augustinianism produces a tradition allegedly able to resolve problems unresolvable in both of its predecessors.

He would later retract that claim and admit that you could not prove the superiority of any of the alternatives. In *Three Rival Versions of Moral Enquiry* (1991), MacIntyre backed away from claiming that you could prove the superiority of one version. He contrasts the ninth edition of the Encyclopedia Britannica, the idea of pure unencumbered rationality, Nietzsche's Genealogy of Morals, the idea that such rationality is simply another expression of the will to power, and Pope Leo XIII's *Aeterni patris*, which sought to establish Thomism as the official doctrine of the Roman Catholic Church. Each of these traditions has irresolvable internal problems. Specifically, Leo XIII misunderstood Thomism by building in a modernist program – of treating Thomism as an epistemological theory like an Encyclopedia rather than as a coherent metaphysical and moral system. MacIntyre rejects any God's-eye neutral nonpartisan interpretation as an illusion. Genuine rational inquiry requires membership in a particular type of moral community.

its myriad forms, we do see a need to hold both faith and reason in high esteem. The tradition of faith and reason is most commendable and reaches back into the middle ages and the *Summa* of Thomas Aquinas and others who were both first-rate thinkers and persons of spiritual depth. A theistic evolution is certainly most plausible as articulated by the likes of Cambridge paleontologist Simon Conway Morris, the award-winning scientist John Pollinghorn, or the director of the National Institutes of Health, biologist Francis Collins.

We are not going to get into all of the details of the conflict between Darwinists and Creationists except to point out that (a) there are serious scientific shortcomings in Darwin's own account even when supplemented by genetics, (b) contemporary neo-Darwinists have a not so-hidden political agenda,[9] and (c) we have already indicated that scientism is not capable of providing an intellectually persuasive or personally satisfying grand narrative. Those who believe that God created the world are not obliged to be Biblical fundamentalists or to defend a particular theory within biology. Christianity can be pro-science without being pro-scientism. There is no conflict between science and religion; there is most definitely a conflict between the philosophical-scientistic narrative and the religious narrative, specifically Christianity.

What is the nature of "disbelief"? "Disbelief" cannot be characterized as the failure of religion to meet certain rational criteria because those very criteria (scientism of the Enlightenment Project) have themselves been de-legitimated. "Disbelief" cannot be characterized as the knowledge that there is no ultimate human meaning; no one is in a position to "know" this, and any "meaning" that there could be has to be "human" in some sense – that is the implication of the Copernican Revolution. Disbelief can only be a moral choice. *It is a moral choice that reflects a kind of personal resentment toward the universe.*

---

9   See the so-called "Darwin Wars" in the works of E. O. Wilson, Dawkins, Dennett, and Pinker vs. Stephen Gould, Lewontin, and Maynard Smith.

We have already called attention to Max Weber as the sociologist who authored *The Protestant Ethics and the Spirit of Capitalism,* a landmark exploration of the relation between religious belief and economic and political activity. But Weber's work also reflected a serious methodological debate with Marxists and others. In the nineteenth century, many social theorists thought of themselves as scientists and began to model their disciplines after the physical sciences. Physical science, it was alleged, explained surface phenomena by appeal to invisible underlying structures (atoms, molecules, genes, etc.). Hence, social science should explain people's thoughts, feelings, and actions by reference to hidden structures (Freud's "subconscious," Marx's "class," etc.). Weber, on the contrary, contended that our consciously held beliefs were not mere epiphenomena driven by subterranean forces but the real causes of why people behave as they do. Spiritual beliefs were among the most important such beliefs.

It is our contention that Weber was correct in this respect. To begin with, neither social science nor artificial intelligence nor brain physiologists have ever succeeded in explaining anything by reference to hidden structures – all we ever get is a succession of fashionable concepts – none of which sticks! Second, the non-Weberian reductive form of social science is unable to make sense of norms or values. All one can say on the non-Weberian account is that so-and-so holds certain beliefs because of such-and-such hidden forces. The latest incarnation of this approach is to dismiss mystical and near-death experiences as aberrations of the brain.

Reductionism is an approach to understanding the nature of complex things by reducing them to the interactions of their parts, or to simpler or more fundamental things. It is a philosophical position that a complex system is nothing but the sum of its parts, and that an account of it can be reduced to accounts of individual constituents.

Religious reductionism generally consists of explaining religion by boiling it down to certain nonreligious causes. A few examples of reductionist attempts to explain the presence of religion are: the view that religion could be reduced to humanity's conceptions of right and wrong; the belief that religion is fundamentally a primitive attempt at controlling our environments, or in the opinion of religion, as a way to explain the existence of the physical world.

There is often a large degree of reductionism in the social sciences, which try to explain whole areas of social activity as mere subfields of their own field. As an example, Marxist economists often try to explain politics as subordinated to the economy, and sociologists see the economy and politics as mere subspheres of society or social forces. Reductionism is always problematic because by definition it reduces reality and distorts it.

It is never possible on this kind of approach even to say that a culture or institution or practice embodies certain values – we can only say that specific individuals pay lip service to certain values but really the underlying forces do all the work; moreover, no one set of underlying forces can legitimate anything on the conscious level. "We are all victims of hidden forces beyond individual control." Of course, many of us indulge in this kind of explanation of those we dislike but somehow manage to exempt ourselves from the process. Aside from the inconsistency, this kind of rhetoric leads to a world in which everybody now dismisses everybody else with whom they disagree. In short, the non-Weberian approach has led to the *end of civil discourse* and argumentation on social issues. The near total politicization of the *news* in all media is but one manifestation of this. The total politicization of the university is another! Finally, part of the revival of the literature on spirituality is a response to an intellectual world devoid of the things that help us to make sense of the world, ourselves, and the relation of ourselves to the world – namely, our consciously held beliefs about what is important to us.

Because of the foregoing, we believe that attempts to defend the *total* rationality of spirituality or religious beliefs are misguided. Such attempts are misguided because they appeal to the very epistemological assumptions that proponents of scientism hold. But those assumptions are ultimately indefensible. It is unnecessary, futile, and self-defeating to engage in this kind of defense. This does not mean that narratives are simply matter of ir-rational or a-rational faith; narratives can contain within themselves very rich and complex arguments and intellectual structures – but they are not just intellectual.

Spirituality in general, and some religions in particular, are narratives that many people have chosen to embrace. The choice cannot be dismissed as thoughtless; it can only be explained ultimately as a choice (like all other narratives) made by a being with free will who chooses to embrace the world in a certain way. This choice is not nihilistic or relativistic. Nevertheless, we are likely to be accused of flirting with or promoting moral relativism or the denying that there is an objective canonical moral truth or a canonical normative account of a subjective truth, or reducing spirituality to aesthetics or historicism. Nothing could be further from the truth, but the mere fact that such a suspicion is entertained evidences our claim that there is a more fundamental misunderstanding. We are not denying the possibility of moral truth. What we are claiming is that the contemporary world is marked by a moral pluralism that reflects two things: (a) the impossibility of resolving moral controversies by sound rational argument based on generally available *secular* moral premises, and (b) that true moral knowledge presupposes a *personal transformation of the knower*. What we are suggesting is that we must take seriously *the limits of discursive moral epistemology*.

Moral epistemic skepticism is not the same as metaphysical moral skepticism. Moral epistemic skepticism acknowledges the limits of resolving moral controversies through sound rational argument; metaphysical moral skepticism doubts whether there is moral truth; one can be skeptical about discursive moral rationality's ability to establish a canonical moral understanding without being a metaphysical moral skeptic.

With the exception of this sentence, every sentence in this book will be challenged by someone or other. That is one reason why we have stressed the importance of narrative. There are competing narratives of just about everything, nor should we be surprised by this given what we have said about the limits of discursive reason. This is not a problem to be overcome; it is instead a reflection of the human condition. Questions of fact aside, anyone who challenges this narrative should not pretend that they are engaging in a merely scholarly exercise. Any challenge to this narrative that claims to be intellectually honest and to maintain intellectual integrity must be or presuppose another narrative.

One additional purpose of this book is to identify and flush out these other narratives, to make critics put all their cards on the table. No doubt there are individuals who have merely negative (or positive) feelings or sentiments about our narrative rather than thoughts, and their position, if you can call it that, remains no more than a series of complaints (or compliments) rather than a serious intellectual alternative. These are the intellectual lost souls or possibly the victims of a half-grasped alternative narrative. More importantly, once having identified alternative narratives we need to acknowledge that believing in a narrative is ultimately a matter of choice, a choice to engage the world in a particular way. We are not therefore simply debating alternative views; we are all (except for the lost souls) advocating a particular way of life. We shall not permit ideology to masquerade as scholarship.

So, in the end, what must be offered in addition to one's own narrative is a grand meta-narrative that takes the possibility of the existence of alterative narratives into account, that is coherent with our understanding of human freedom (autonomy), that does not rest upon or terminate in relativism, that is nevertheless compatible with individuals personally holding a wide variety of (but not all) metaphysical and religious positions.

There will not be agreement on the grand meta-narrative. Nevertheless, all parties to the discussion are required to present one. Failure to present one shows that (a) either you have failed to understand the preceding arguments, or that (b) your lower-level narrative lacks the resources to deal with conflict, or that (c) you are *unwilling* to subscribe to a system of purely procedural norms for policy purposes, and therefore harbor the intent to impose your own substantive views. Not to offer a meta-narrative more often than not reflects the typical inability or unwillingness to think through one's own position – perhaps a refusal to lay one's cards on the table; to refuse to do so is in the end not to be able to understand the position of others who do offer a full articulation of their position – and therefore incapacitates one for reaching a meaningful resolution; to offer a meta-narrative that contravenes autonomy is to flirt with threats to liberty.

We have not (and cannot) offer a complete theoretical justification of our grand meta-narrative. We have offered theoretical reasons that make diversity intelligible but do not require the de-legitimation of most moral communities (which are enterprise associations). This account preserves dignity, autonomy, identity, and encourages recognition. On the other hand, we are deeply concerned about some alternative accounts for whom the modern world is an alien place or who feel threatened by diversity and autonomy. What we can do here is to remind everyone that since Locke's *Letter Concerning Toleration*, we have seen that Christianity has the resources to be tolerant. Is that true of other narratives?

The existence of alternative narratives does not entail moral relativism. What we can have is a political consensus on procedural norms only supplemented with the recognition that substantive moral views are housed within narratives on which there is not likely to be consensus. The only limitation on such substantive moral views is that they make provision for the fact that there is a plurality of narratives and that agreement can only be secured on the procedural norms. This is precisely the way in which the seventeenth and eighteenth centuries resolved the religious-political question. There is no reason why that kind of resolution cannot be achieved today. Oakeshott's distinction between civil association and enterprise association is helpful here. An enterprise association has a common/collective goal; a civic association does not. Modern states are civil associations within which we as individuals are free to voluntarily join a host of institutions that are or might be enterprise associations (e.g., the family, a religious community, etc.). It is only within a larger civil association that multiple enterprise associations can flourish.

Whatever one's substantive narrative, it cannot be a direct part of politics. There can only be a private moral and/or religious narrative; there cannot be an official moral/religious narrative. This limitation, coupled with the fact that there is no consensus moral/religious narrative, but a plurality of such narratives, means that we must tolerate all narratives that involve recognition of this limitation. This further entails that a definition of what constitutes an evil to be suppressed by the state cannot be defined in wholly religious terms. Organized religions may speak out against anything they consider immoral and they should be allowed to refuse to participate in any such activity or to subsidize it. This is also a reason to limit the state!

This helps to illuminate the spiritual culture wars of the present and foreseeable future.

A. Enlightenment Project secular democratic socialism (current version of the Rousseau/Marx narrative): commitment to techno-efficiency, consumerism, and self-indulgence. Human beings are considered as merely material beings, higher forms of animal life, whose ultimate goal is to live as long and as comfortably as possible. They would advocate public policies that prioritize the commitment to health care, liberal sexual emancipation, and living longer or postponing death indefinitely.

B. Judeo-Christian Narrative: recognize the sanctity of human life. We question whether this moral insight will survive the loss of belief in a cosmic narrative. A new lease on life has been given to Christianity, one which provides for it a space as a kind of counter-culture rather than as the dominant culture. Much of our ethics makes little sense outside of a Judeo-Christian context. Neo-Christianity, in whatever forms it takes, will no longer command the political heights. This has long been true of Judaism. But many would argue that this is a better form of Christianity, i.e., more secure from corruption, more fulfilling, less likely to breed the larger cultural cynicism that saps the strength both of the culture and Christianity itself.

C. Other orthodox religious or polytheistic positions and cultural traditions which reject the logic of acquisitive materialism in favor of some vague form of spirituality.

D. Those who recognize and want the special moral function of the Judeo-Christian tradition (as well as other major religious traditions) but cannot bring themselves to embrace religion. Most of the major Protestant theologians of the twentieth century including Barth, Bultmann, Jaspers, and Tillich had caved in to positivism and turned to faith alone as a justification of Christianity.[10] The death of God movement in the 1960s[11] officially marks for Protestantism the onset of a post-Christian era characterized by a kind of religious atheism, or what Louis Dupré has called a form of humanism beyond atheism.

E. Star Trek/E.T.: Those who remain committed to the Enlightenment Project because we cannot see any other, recognize its intellectual shortcomings, and substitute for those shortcomings recognition of a vague and generic sense of spirituality. It promotes the emergence of generic chaplains who facilitate a vague sense of spiritual fulfillment. Human finitude is now reconciled by a vague mystical spirituality without particular content. However, because of its lack of specific content, this new spirituality is compatible with all of the horrendous policies of the Enlightenment Project.

The Enlightenment Project accepted the core values of the Judeo-Christian world view (in updated liberal-secular terms) but attempted to justify those values by appeal to science. If scientism is jettisoned, the only course available is to interpret and defend those values in sui generis fashion. French intellectuals

---

10　Karl Jaspers, *Philosophie* (1931); Bultmann and Tillich were influenced by Heidegger's *Being and Time*.
11　See Gabriel Vahanian, *The Death of God* (1960); Bishop John A.T. Robinson, *Honest to God* (1963); see also the works of Thomas Altizer and Paul Van Buren.

do this with all kinds of rhetorical flourish, Rorty uses the language of pragmatism, humanists use profane religious rhetoric, and so-called professional philosophers use trendy versions of Kant, utilitarianism, or virtue ethics. In practice this amounts to no more than the masking of private political and social agendas. But the only common meta-principle at which they have arrived is to appeal to the toleration of different perspectives. The problem is that this begs the question: How are we to understand toleration? Locke's view of toleration was at least based on a substantive commitment to Christianity, whereas the general contemporary trend is to base it on relativism; the only real argument is a prudential-Hobbesian one,[12] namely it keeps the peace so that we can go about our business of being Nietzschean lastmen. To begin with, this argument does not convince religious extremists (who advocate a world-wide enterprise association, e.g., Al Qaida); second, the relativistic argument is ultimately nihilist. Moreover, the prudential argument is rhetorical not substantive; a procedural norm without a substantive norm will not survive.

We need to recognize both the necessity for agreement only on the procedural level and the necessity for providing a metanarrative (it does not have to be the same for everyone but it must perform the function) that supports the agreement on the procedural level. If not, we shall be driven to rationalize a secular morality as substantive public policy. The need to justify policy coupled with the inevitability of moral epistemological relativism will drive us in the direction of imposing a universal secular morality. Since the only thing on which there can be agreement is procedural norms, and since procedural norms embody a wholly instrumental thinking, a bio-technical instrumentalism becomes the reigning SUBSTANTIVE VIEW. It can only see human beings as having physical needs like avoiding pain. By identifying people solely with their bodies, it enslaves them to their

---

12 John Gray, 1991. "Postscript: After Liberalism," pp. 239–66 in *Liberalisms*. London: Routledge.

bodies and promotes a culture in which autonomy is absent. Envy is present only where autonomy is not. Instead of liberating us, it enslaves us to a materialist conception of the human predicament. The threat is that there might eventually be no diversity. The denial of an official religion has progressed into the advocacy of a secular system in which religious practices at odds with the secular agenda are denied legitimacy as well as funding. Militant secularism presents itself here not as one alternative but as a substantive view to be imposed upon all. What emerges is a self-righteous and messianic secularism. It justifies itself by saying it is in favor of toleration, but in practice it becomes an intolerant advocate of a reductivist and materialist way of life. Finally, statism is both a threat to civil association and a specific threat to religious communities.

Conclusion

There is a natural progression from centralization to secularism, from secularism to materialism, and from materialism to a social-collectivist conception of human welfare, that is, the standard social-democratic view in which inequalities are considered bad in themselves. We assert that the welfare state undermines institutions (e.g., family and religion) that promote spiritual capital; militant secularism as a quasi-religion promotes a reductive conception of human nature, one that denies freedom and responsibility. We already see the results full blown in the impoverishment and implosion of the Communist empire and we are seeing the gradual evisceration of spiritual capital in Western Europe. For these reasons, we ask the question: What is the future of Spiritual Capital in America? Is American spiritual capital being eroded? It is time to retrieve, restate, and revitalize America's spiritual capital?

AFTERTHOUGHTS

1. America was both settled and founded by people who took the Bible (the Old *and* New Testaments) as their serious starting point.

2. Every aspect of America's culture is permeated by language and ideas that are derived from the Bible. Think of Lincoln's *Gettysburg Address* and Martin Luther King's *I Have a Dream*.

3. It is this Judeo-Christian spiritual capital that makes it possible for people of other faiths or, in fact, no faith to flourish and to contribute to American culture.

4. America is a profoundly Judeo-Christian culture, and we should not be afraid to affirm and reaffirm it as a historical fact and as an on-going reality.

5. The origin of the belief in the dignity and equality of individual human beings is the unique Biblical assertion that man is created in God's *image,* and the *Bible* was the inspiration for the abolition of slavery and the dignity of all persons.

6. Limited government was first proclaimed in the *Torah*. And it was Jesus who said, "render unto Caesar the things that are Caesar's, and to God the things that are God's."

7. Judeo-Christian spiritual capital encourages Americans to be the most philanthropic people on the earth. Whenever a major disaster occurs anywhere in the world, the first telephone call or request for help begins with "1."

8. The presence of self-proclaimed Christians who are immoral does *not* invalidate America's spiritual capital; the presence of moral individuals who proclaim no commitment, does not show that the entire society can survive a lack of spiritual capital.

9. At no point in its history has the world been free of barbarism. It is difficult to understand how barbarism can be actively opposed by people without faith in something or belief in the rightness and goodness of their way of life and human flourishing.

10. To the extent that religious freedom, economic freedom, and political freedom exist anywhere in the world it is because of the role that America's spiritual capital has played prior to and especially since 1941. Calling America a superpower is to put on social-scientific blinders that obfuscate its true spiritual capital.

ACKNOWLEDGMENTS

Truth be known this book was born in the City of Brotherly Love. That is the case because both of the authors claim that beloved place as their city of birth. Although separated by over a decade in years, a set of railroad tracks between classes, and a wall separating Catholics and Protestants, we as authors claim the same heritage. That heritage we are proud to say is Judeo-Christian and it was born in our city some 250 years ago and in the call for Independence.

The Founders declared that faith in Philadelphia, in words and deeds. American leadership grew on the very streets we grew up on and in the halls, malls, and taverns nearby. Flags were sown in her alleys and navies raised on her rivers. Battles were won in nearby fields. In waves of immigration later peoples came from all corners of the world for a single reason, and that can be summed up in one word: freedom.

One of us is of Italian ancestry and the other Scottish and Dutch, but it matters not. Our fathers fought in repeated wars to maintain America's freedom and we continued that fight as cold warriors against the ills of godless communism. Our lives are vastly different stories with education the common thread that brought us together. In forums, colloquia, and research our interests converged and this book was born.

It was born out of necessity. As we came to gauge the loss of spiritual capital in our homeland, we came to appreciate that we have been losing ground. But we believe it is not too late to revive it. With collectivization and the therapeutic state on the rise, we thought it time again to restate loudly and clearly, as the original Liberty Bell itself rang, the sound and saga of American freedom.

We need to thank all our many mentors and friends who have taught us, argued with us, and coaxed us into this project. It is a product of equals. One of us is a political economist and the other trained in philosophy. We are friends and we think alike. The Templeton Foundation helped fund some of the research that led to the writing of this book; and our editors have proven most wise in its rendering. We are responsible for its argument and any errors of omission or commission.

This book started as a conversation some three years ago. We were in our hometown for a *Philadelphia Society* meeting and staying across from Independence Hall. We were deciding where to grab a bite to eat, and thought, "Why not have a great Philly cheese steak?" Well, in America there is only one place to get a "real" cheese steak and of course that is Philadelphia. So we were on the right track. But where? Naturally, after some debate, we settled on South Philadelphia and the home of two of the best cheese steaks known to man. On one corner—literally cattycorner to each other – are Pat's and Gino's.

The two establishments may serve the same products but they differ vastly in style and substance. And it was this fact that began this book. *Choice*. America is, we think built on choice. It is uniquely grounded in religious-economic-and political freedom. We made the diplomatic decision to have one of each – what is more American? We needed to conduct research so as to be able to compare the differences and to savor the distinctions. Why not? And in that process we started what became a profound conversation that gave rise to this very book.

So thank you for the cheese steaks and to all those who shaped and kept America free; to our lovely wives and families, to friends and critics both. Let freedom ring . . . and keep ringing
. . .

Our specific thanks ring out to Acton Institute, The Templeton Foundation, especially, Arthur Schwartz and Kimon Sargeant, Joe Johnston, our mentor, Liberty Fund, The Bradley Foundation, The Federalist Society, Ken Grasso, Loyola University, and its new Center on Spiritual Capital, Bill Campbell and the Philadelphia Society, and Yale's Center for Faith & Culture, which houses the Spiritual Capital Initiative.

ABOUT THE AUTHORS

Nicholas Capaldi is *Legendre-Soulé Distinguished Chair in Business Ethics* at Loyola University, New Orleans. He also serves as Director of the Center for Spiritual Capital. He taught previously at: the University of Tulsa where he was McFarlin Research Professor of Law; Columbia University; Queens College, City University of New York; The United States Military Academy at West Point, and the National University of Singapore. He was a national fellow at the Hoover Institution in 1979-80, the year that it served as Reagan's think tank.

Professor Capaldi received his B.A. from the University of Pennsylvania and his Ph.D. from Columbia University. His principal research and teaching interest is in public policy and its intersection with political science, philosophy, law, religion, and economics. He is the author of seven books, over 80 articles, and editor of six anthologies. He is a member of the editorial board of six journals and has served most recently as editor of *Public Affairs Quarterly. He is actively involved with Intercollegiate Studies Institute, Liberty Fund, The Federalist Society, CATO, Heritage Foundation, AEI, IEA, APEE, and serves on the Board of the Philadelphia Society.*

Capaldi is the recipient of grants from the National Endowment for the Humanities, The Mellon Foundation, The U.S. Department of Education, The Board of Regents of Louisiana, and the John Templeton Foundation, among others. He is an internationally recognized scholar and a domestic public policy specialist on such issues as higher education, bio-ethics, business ethics, affirmative action, and immigration.

Recent publications by Professor Capaldi's include articles on corporate social responsibility, the ethics of free market societies, and an intellectual biography of John Stuart Mill in connection with which he was recently interviewed on C-SPAN's *Booknotes.*

Theodore Roosevelt Malloch is a Research professor at Yale University, and Chairman and Chief Executive officer of The Roosevelt Group, a leading strategic management and thought leadership company. He has served on the executive board of the World Economic Forum, which hosts the renowned annual Davos meeting in Switzerland. He held an ambassadorial level position in the United Nations in Geneva during the period when the Berlin wall collapsed and the cold war ended.

Malloch has been a Senior Fellow of the Aspen Institute, where he previously directed all of its national seminars. He was also President of the CNN World Economic Development Congress that focused on "building the integrated global economy" attended by 2500 international CEOs, Ministers of Governments, investment, and economic leaders. At that meeting Margaret Thatcher dubbed him "a global *sherpa.*" He has worked with Salomon Brothers on Wall Street, as head of consulting and research for Wharton Econometrics, and has held senior positions in the US State Department and the US Senate Committee on Foreign Relations. He has taught at a number of leading colleges and universities and appears frequently on television and in print.

An accomplished author, his most recent books are: *Spiritual Enterprise: Doing Virtuous Business*, Encounter Books 2008 and *Renewing American Culture: The Pursuit of Happiness*, 2006, with Scott Massey, which has been made into an Emmy-nominated PBS documentary.

Malloch serves on several corporate, mutual fund and not-for-profit boards, including Yale Divinity School, University of Toronto International Governing Council, a Pew Charitable Trust board, the Templeton Foundation; and as an advisor to many think tanks including, The Hudson Institute, American Foreign Policy Council, and the Social Affairs Unit in the UK.

Ted earned his Ph.D. in international political economy from the University of Toronto where he studied on a Hart House open fellowship. He took his BA from Gordon College and an M.Litt. from an ancient Scottish university as a St. Andrew's Society scholar. He was awarded an honorary LL.D. degree from the University of Aberdeen in 2008. He recently founded and is Chairman of the new *Spiritual Enterprise Institute*, which focuses on the virtue of spiritual capital. He is active in the Episcopal Church and has been knighted into both the Templar and the Order of St. John.

INDEX